Spelling Matters

3rd Edition

Andrew J Woods

Pearson Australia
(a division of Pearson Australia Group Pty Ltd)
707 Collins Street, Melbourne, Victoria 3008
PO Box 23360, Melbourne, Victoria 8012
www.pearson.com.au

First published 1993
Second edition 2002
Third edition 2008

2018 2017 2016 2015
12 11 10 9

Editor: Frith Luton
Text designer: Meaghan Barbuto
Typesetter: Anita Adams and Eugenio Fazio
Cover designer: Meaghan Barbuto
Cover illustration: Photolibrary Pty Ltd
Illustrations: Luke Jurevicius
Printed and bound in Australia by Pegasus Media & Logistics

Pearson Australia Group Pty Ltd ABN 40 004 245 943

Acknowledgements
The publishers wish to thank the following organisations who kindly gave permission to reproduce copyright material in this book:
A.A. Milne, *When We Were Very Young*. © The Trustees of the Pooh Properties. Published by Egmont UK Ltd London and used with permission: p. 31.

Contents

Introduction

Welcome to *Spelling Matters Book 3*.

The *Spelling Matters* series has been developed to allow both the classroom teacher and parents to improve students' word attack skills and vocabulary range. The series provides exercises for use in the classroom and at home.

This book contains 40 work units (36 Classroom and Home Study Units and four Review Units).

The Classroom Unit

At the beginning of each unit a list of words is provided. The words in this list have a phonological, visual, morphemic or etymological relationship to each other. The Classroom Unit is a series of exercises designed to develop phonological, visual and (in the Word Building section) morphemic knowledge. Challenge words are provided at the end of each unit for vocabulary extension.

The Home Study Unit

The Home Study Unit should be completed at home, and parents are encouraged to assist their children with this unit.

The quotation, proverb or rhyme at the top of each unit shows how words from the lists have been used in our language.

The exercises in each Home Study Unit are similar in nature to those found in the Classroom Unit, although more word puzzle activities are provided.

Word Knowledge is aimed at further developing students' etymological knowledge and encourages experimentation with language.

The General Knowledge section demonstrates that the list and challenge words are not just 'spelling words', but important elements of our language. This component of each unit should provide both parent and child with a stimulating 'sharing' time. Students should be encouraged to seek help to complete this section if necessary, thereby involving parents directly in Home Study assignments.

Optional testing

If teachers choose to test students, a weekly test can be administered. This should be a random selection of ten list words. For those students seeking an extra challenge, a choice of Challenge words could be tested.

A record of students' progress may be kept using the Student Profile on page 92.

Also provided, at the back of the book, is:

- a glossary of terms used in the units of work. Words included in the Glossary are shown in bold throughout the book.
- a Spelling Reference List containing all the List and Challenge words used in the 40 units. This list can be used by teachers, parents and students as another means of checking mastery of words.

A final note

Because language develops at different rates, students may not necessarily need to work at specified levels. Some teachers may wish to select isolated units of work related to a particular student's area of weakness.

Remember that spelling and vocabulary development should be associated with a variety of language experiences and should therefore be integrated into a total learning program.

Andrew Woods

How to use Spelling Matters

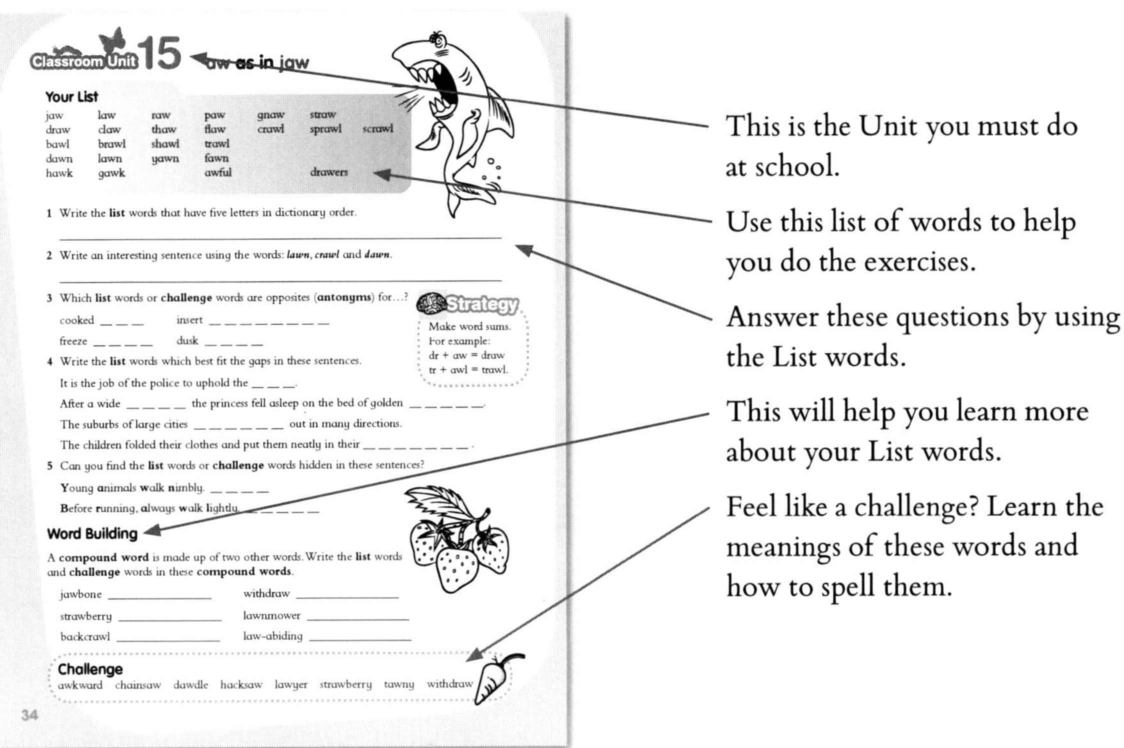

Classroom Unit 15 aw as in jaw

Your List

jaw law raw paw gnaw straw
draw claw thaw flaw crawl sprawl scrawl
bawl brawl shawl trawl
dawn lawn yawn fawn
hawk gawk awful drawers

1 Write the **list** words that have five letters in dictionary order.

2 Write an interesting sentence using the words: ***lawn, crawl*** and ***dawn***.

3 Which **list** words or **challenge** words are opposites (**antonyms**) for...?

cooked _ _ _ insert _ _ _ _ _ _ _ _

freeze _ _ _ _ dusk _ _ _ _

Strategy
Make word sums.
For example:
dr + aw = draw
tr + awl = trawl.

4 Write the **list** words which best fit the gaps in these sentences.

It is the job of the police to uphold the _ _ _.

After a wide _ _ _ _ the princess fell asleep on the bed of golden _ _ _ _ _.

The suburbs of large cities _ _ _ _ _ _ _ out in many directions.

The children folded their clothes and put them neatly in their _ _ _ _ _ _ _ _.

5 Can you find the **list** words or **challenge** words hidden in these sentences?

Young animals walk nimbly. _ _ _ _

Before running, always walk lightly. _ _ _ _ _

Word Building

A **compound word** is made up of two other words. Write the **list** words and **challenge** words in these **compound words**.

jawbone ______ withdraw ______

strawberry ______ lawnmower ______

backcrawl ______ law-abiding ______

Challenge
awkward chainsaw dawdle hacksaw lawyer strawberry tawny withdraw

34

This is the Unit you must do at school.

Use this list of words to help you do the exercises.

Answer these questions by using the List words.

This will help you learn more about your List words.

Feel like a challenge? Learn the meanings of these words and how to spell them.

Can you find the List or Challenge word?

This work must be done at home. Ask your parents to help you with it.

Try using the new words you find in this section when you next write a story, a letter, or in your diary or journal.

You may need to use reference books to help you with this section. Perhaps Mum, Dad or someone else could help.

Home Study Unit 15

It is the last straw that breaks the camel's back. (Proverb)

1 Which **list** words would fit into these Wordframes?

2 Draw a fawn and a hawk see-sawing on a lawn.

3 Write meanings for these **list** words. A dictionary may help.

gnaw ______

shawl ______

flaw ______

Word Knowledge

A trawler is a type of fishing boat. Can you explain why it might be called a trawler?

General Knowledge

1 I am the name given to the young of a deer. ______

2 Who am I? I was a famous Australian writer. I wrote such stories as 'The Loaded Dog' and 'The Drover's Wife'.

H _ _ _ _ L _ _ _ _ _

3 Who am I? I was an Antarctic explorer. My name is used for one of Australia's Antarctic bases.

D _ _ _ _ _ _ M _ _ _ _ _

35

If you are unsure of a word's meaning, look in the Glossary on page 94.
All of the words in this book can be found in the Spelling Reference List beginning on page 86. Tick the words that you can spell.
Answers are provided at the end of this book.

The magic e: a _ e

Your List

face	make	mate	wade	name	wage	cave
race	bake	date	fade	same	rage	wave
lace	take	gate	made	came	cage	gave
space	cake	hate	shade	game	page	save
place	snake	late	grade	flame	stage	brave

1 Which **list** words rhyme with…?

ace ____________ ____________ ____________ ____________ ____________

state ____________ ____________ ____________ ____________ ____________

2 Write these words in dictionary order: ***cage***, ***fade***, ***bake***, ***gave*** and ***date***.

____

3 Which **list** words best match these groups?

nose mouth eyes ____________ rocket planet star ____________

friend pal buddy ____________ paddle swim bathe ____________

4 Which **list** words fit into the gaps in these sentences?

Lee was asked to turn to _ _ _ _ sixteen of his workbook.

When the show ended, the actors quickly left the _ _ _ _ _.

The surfer used the huge _ _ _ _ to speed to the beach.

Word Building

1 To add ***ing*** to the following words, the ***e*** must be dropped.
For example: date + *ing* = dating.

race + ing = ________________ wave + ing = ________________

make + ing = ________________ take + ing = ________________

save + ing = ________________ shade + ing = ________________

2 A **compound word** is a word that is made up of two other words.
Add **list** words to these to make **compound words**.

__________ ship check __________

__________ way shock __________

Challenge

became	educate
embrace	engage
enrage	invade
locate	mistake
parade	surname

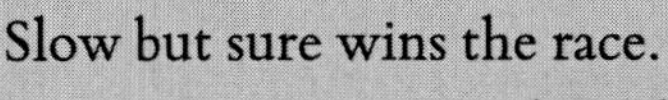

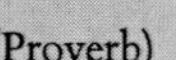

1 Write these **list** words in dictionary order: ***snake***, ***shade***, ***stage*** and ***space***.

____

2 Complete this Wordsearch by finding the **list** words.

bake	race
cake	shade
face	snake
make	space
place	take

S	D	E	C	A	R	P	S	T	A	H
C	H	A	T	A	K	E	P	R	I	M
E	K	A	C	P	P	L	A	C	E	A
C	J	K	D	E	A	C	C	W	K	K
A	C	A	K	E	H	A	E	L	A	E
F	G	S	N	A	K	E	T	R	B	I

Look:
horizontally ⟷
vertically ↕
diagonally ⤢ ⤡

3 Which **list** words mean…?

cook in an oven ____________ without fear ____________

strongly dislike ____________ not on time ____________

4 Write today's date on this line. ____________________

Word Knowledge

1 Which **list** words do you think these words come from?

cavern ____________ facial ____________ outrageous ____________

hatred ____________ inflammable ____________ surname ____________

2 Choose three **challenge** words. Find their meanings and then write one sentence containing all of them.

____

____

____

General Knowledge

1 What kind of animal do the following words describe? tiger, brown, taipan ____________

2 Name a lake in the state where you live. ____________________

3 Circle which of the following can be used in the garden:

cake rake stake brake rate spade lame

2 The magic e: ale as in pale

Your List

ale	pale	gale	sale	tale
male	whale	stale	scale	female

Strategy

Look for smaller words.
For example: pale = ale
stale = tale

1 Which **list** words are hidden in these **acrostics**?

Tigers always lick everybody. ____________ Men are like emus. ____________

2 ***Sale*** means the selling of goods for money. ***Sail*** means to travel on water or a large sheet used for catching the wind. Write each word in a sentence.

____

____

3 Which **list** words are opposites (**antonyms**) for these words?

fresh _ _ _ _ _ bright _ _ _ _ male _ _ _ _ _ _ _

4 Complete the following:

Male means ____

____

Mail means ____

____

5 ***Tale*** means a story. ***Tail*** means the end of the backbone.
Write a sentence for each word.

____

____

Word Building

Make new words by adding the words in Column A to those in Column B.

Column A		Column B		New Words
whole	+	sale	=	____________
stale	+	mate	=	____________
whale	+	bone	=	____________
tell	+	tale	=	____________
full	+	scale	=	____________

Challenge

exhale
inhale
nightingale

Home Study Unit 2

A tale never loses in the telling.
(Proverb)

1 Write these words in dictionary order: ***gale***, ***sale***, ***female*** and ***ale***.

____

2 Write an interesting sentence containing: ***pale*** and ***male***.

____

3 Which **list** words or **challenge** words mean the same as…?

a windy storm ____________ a story ____________

a songbird ____________ breathe out ____________

4 Find all of the **list** words in this Wordsearch.

A	F	L	E	A	P	A	I	L	M
L	I	E	S	A	A	I	S	L	A
E	F	E	M	L	L	E	T	S	L
A	S	A	T	A	E	G	A	L	E
S	A	L	E	A	L	M	L	A	I
W	I	W	H	A	L	E	E	L	L
A	L	S	C	A	L	E	S	A	L

Word Knowledge

bale, meaning to scoop out water, can also be spelt _ _ _ _.

bale, meaning to jump from an aeroplane, can also be spelt _ _ _ _.

bale, meaning a package such as a bale of wool, can only be spelt _ _ _ _.

General Knowledge

1 The Beaufort Scale measures the strength of the wind.

Which **list** word do you think might appear on the Beaufort Scale? _ _ _ _

2 What am I? I am a breed of working dog from England's Aire River valley.

I am the largest terrier. ____________

3 The magic e: i _ e

Your List

line	vine	dine	pine	nine	fine	mine	wine
spine	twine	swine	shine	whine	shrine		
pipe	wipe	ripe	swipe	stripe	while		

1 Write these words in dictionary order: ***line***, ***pine***, ***vine*** and ***nine***.

____

2 Match these meanings with **list** words:

ready to harvest _ _ _ _

to have dinner _ _ _ _

to rub clean _ _ _ _

a hollow tube _ _ _ _

backbone _ _ _ _ _

to hit (or hit at) hard _ _ _ _ _

3 Use each of these **list** words in an interesting sentence.

twine ______________________________

shrine ______________________________

4 ***Whine*** and ***wine*** are **homophones** — words that sound the same as another word but have a different spelling and a different meaning. Write the correct words in these gaps.

All the customer did for the entire meal was __________ about the taste of the __________.

5 The word ***mine*** is a **homograph** — a word that has two different meanings, although it sounds the same, and is spelt the same.

Write two sentences that show the different meanings of ***mine***.

____

____

(One name for both **homophones** and **homographs** is **homonyms**.)

Word Building

Use words from the **list** to build new words.

A compound word made up of two fruits. _ _ _ _ a p p l e

Add the **suffix** ***ty*** to me to increase my number by ten times.

_ _ _ _ t y

Add the **suffix** ***al*** to me, drop the e and I mean 'of the backbone'.

_ _ _ _ a l

Challenge

canine	decline
define	divine
feline	gripe
incline	intestine
snipe	tripe
turbine	viper

A stitch in time saves nine.
(Proverb)

1 Write these words in dictionary order: ***pipe***, ***ripe***, ***wipe*** and ***wine***.

____

2 Which of the **list** or **challenge** words mean…?

pigs ____________ an engine ____________

a snake ____________ a body organ ____________

3 Use the clues and the **list** words to complete this Crossword.

Across
1 thin string
4 a type of tree
5 a creeping plant

Down
2 to rub clean
3 the number before ten

		1	2		3	
				■		
			4			
5						

Word Knowledge

Brine is water that is strongly salted.

Therefore sea water can be described as the _ _ _ _ _ sea.

General Knowledge

1 Can you match these words with their meanings?
For example: *canine* means like a dog.

serpentine		a tiger
feline		a lion
elephantine		a horse
leonine	like	a cat
equine		an elephant
porcine		a pig
tigrine		a serpent

2 How is the rank of sergeant shown on an army uniform?

____

____

Classroom Unit 4 The magic e: ore as in core

Your List

ore	wore	core	bore	tore	sore	more	fore
score	store	shore	snore	chore	ashore	restore	explore

1 Which **list** words mean…?

a job _ _ _ _ _ to put back or bring back _ _ _ _ _ _ _

front _ _ _ _ a mined rock or mineral _ _ _

painful _ _ _ _ on land _ _ _ _ _ _

beach _ _ _ _ _ middle _ _ _ _

2 Write these **list** words in dictionary order: ***sore***, ***bore***, ***tore***, ***store*** and ***wore***.

____

3 Write a sentence for each of these **homophones**. You may need a dictionary to help you.

wore ______________________________

war ______________________________

shore ______________________________

sure ______________________________

Word Building

Use the clues below to help you make new words with *fore* as a **base word**.

For example: *fore* + most = foremost (first, top, or most important)

fore _ _ _ (between the wrist and elbow)

fore _ _ _ _ (predict or warn about the future)

fore _ _ _ _ _ _ _ (the finger next to the thumb)

fore _ _ _ _ (to have seen something before it happened)

fore _ _ _ _ (front part of head above eyes)

fore _ _ _ _ _ _ _ (front part of a picture)

Strategy

Look
Say
Cover
Write
Check

Challenge

carnivore encore folklore gore herbivore omnivore pore spore

Home Study Unit 4

> The way to be a bore is to say everything.
>
> (Voltaire)

1 Complete this Wordsearch by using the **list** words shown.

S H O R E B R E O R E B K

A C O S C O R E A R W R O

A O E T U O E F O T O R E

S R R P N W S B O L R A N

H E O S A R T R E R E M C

O A T O C H O R E P E V R

R O S O R E R M O R E L D

E X P L O R E A R E R O E

ashore	fore	sore
bore	more	snore
chore	restore	store
core	score	tore
explore	shore	wore

2 Use a dictionary to help you write the difference in meaning of

sore ______________________________

and

soar ______________________________

3 Add the **suffix *ing*** to these **list** words. You must drop the ***e*** before adding the ending.

bore ____________ snore ____________ explore ____________

Word Knowledge

Folk means people. *Lore* means learning or knowledge. Use these meanings to write your own meaning for the word *folklore*.

____

(Check the meaning of folklore in a dictionary to see how close it is to your meaning.)

General Knowledge

What am I?

1 I am a seed. sp _ _ _

2 I am the name for an animal which eats meat.

c _ _ _ _ _ _ _ _ _ e

3 I am the name for an animal which eats plants.

h _ _ _ _ _ _ _ _ _ e

4 I am a little hole in the skin for perspiration.

p _ _ _

5 I eat both meat and plants. o _ _ _ _ _ _ _ e

Classroom Unit 5 The magic e: o _ e

Your List

rose	pose	hose	nose	close	chose	those	arose
hole	pole	mole	whole	stole			
bone	lone	stone	throne	hope	rope	slope	

1 Which **list** words mean the same as…?

shut _ _ _ _ _ rock _ _ _ _ _ slant _ _ _ _ _

post _ _ _ _ total _ _ _ _ _ gap _ _ _ _

2 What am I? Choose answers from the **list** words.

I am used by gardeners and firefighters. _ _ _ _

I am found on a face. _ _ _ _ A dog may enjoy chewing me. _ _ _ _

A royal person might sit on me. _ _ _ _ _ _

I am an underground-living animal. _ _ _ _ I am a flower. _ _ _ _

3 Write the words below in sentences to show that you understand their meanings.

arose ______________________________

lone ______________________________

chose ______________________________

4 Write the **list** words that rhyme with *soap*.

____

5 Which **list** words are **homonyms** for these words?

knows __________ thrown __________ rows __________ loan __________

Word Building

Add the ending (**suffix**) shown, to make new words. For example: dispose + *able* = disposable. (Where the word *careful* appears, you must change the word before adding the ending.)

close + ure (*careful*) ______________________

lone + ly ______________________

hope + ful ______________________

pole + ar (*careful*) ______________________

compose + ure (*careful*) ______________________

expose + ure (*careful*) ______________________

Challenge

antelope
compose
console
cyclone
diagnose
dispose
enclose
expose
glucose
postpone
propose
rissole
trombone

What's in a name? That which we call a rose By any other name would smell as sweet.

(William Shakespeare)

1 Use the **list** words ***close*** and ***rose*** to fill the gaps in these sentences.

'Because you are _ _ _ _ _ to the window, could you please _ _ _ _ _ it?' asked Robin.

The princess _ _ _ _ slowly from her throne and placed

a single red _ _ _ _ on the table.

2 Write the **list** words which rhyme with the word ***moan*** in dictionary order.

____

3 Underline the correct word in these sentences.
The (loan/lone) figure waited while the bank manager approved his (loan/lone).
Ian had not told his mum the (hole/whole) story about the (hole/whole) in the wall.

4 Which **list** word means the opposite (**antonym**) of…?

open _ _ _ _ _ part _ _ _ _ _ gloom _ _ _ _

Word Knowledge

Which **challenge** words are the **base words** for…?

proposal (a suggestion) _ _ _ _ _ _ _ _ _

The manager accepted the director's ______________ of a merger.

consolation (cheer up) _ _ _ _ _ _ _ _ _

Each of the losers was given a red ribbon as a ______________ prize.

disposal (getting rid of) _ _ _ _ _ _ _ _ _

The workers were responsible for the ______________ of the rubbish.

General Knowledge

1 What do the following have in common? Beethoven, Bach, Grainger, Tchaikovsky and Mozart were all _ _ _ _ _ _ _ _ _ _ _.

2 What am I? I am an Olympic athletics event. Athletes must use a piece of equipment to help them leap over an obstacle. _ _ _ _ _ _ _ _ _ _

3 What am I? I am the natural sugar found in plants and used by animals and humans for energy. I am _ _ _ _ _ _ _ _ _ _.

Classroom Unit 6 ee as in seen

Your List

fee	bee	see	beef	deep	been	seem	week	free	glee
creek	need	seek	meet	reed	flee	tree	heed	feed	keen
feet	keep	peep	seed	seen	meek	weep	weed	three	deed

1 Write these **list** words in dictionary order: ***seek***, ***beef***, ***peep***, ***meek*** and ***weed***.

____

2 Write **list** words that sound the same but are spelt differently to these: (These words are called **homophones**.)

I am a green vegetable. _ _ _ _ My list homophone is _ _ _ _.

I am animal flesh. _ _ _ _ My list homophone is _ _ _ _.

I am not strong, I am _ _ _ _. My list homophone is _ _ _ _.

I mean to look at and understand words. _ _ _ _

My **list homophone** is _ _ _ _ .

Strategy

All of the list words contain double *e*.

3 Write an interesting sentence containing: ***free***, ***keep*** and ***three***.

____

4 Which **list** words or **challenge** words mean…?

meat from cattle _ _ _ _ to run away from something _ _ _ _

enthusiastic _ _ _ _ a piece of playground equipment _ _ _-_ _ _

an insect _ _ _ cafeteria _ _ _ _ _ _ _ _

in the middle of two things _ _ _ _ _ _ _

5 Which **list** words begin and end with the same letter?

_______________ _______________

Word Building

Write the **list** or **challenge** words from which these words are built.

gleeful _____________ depth _____________

freedom _____________ wept _____________

excessive _____________ successful _____________

Challenge

between	canteen
exceed	fifteen
indeed	see-saw
succeed	tweezers

Home Study Unit 6

> Laugh and the world laughs with you;
> Weep, and you weep alone.
>
> (Ella Wheeler Wilcox)

1 Write an interesting sentence containing: ***creek***, ***tree*** and ***reed***.

____

2 Match these **homophones** with their correct meanings. (**Homophones** are words which sound alike but are spelt differently and have different meanings.)

reed	a deed of great skill or courage
read	to come face to face with
been	animal flesh
bean	a swamp grass
feet	vegetable
feat	to have existed or to have gone
meet	to look at words and understand them
meat	the parts of the body at the end of the legs

3 Draw a picture of a beefy prisoner fleeing gleefully to freedom.

Word Knowledge

All of the following words have something to do with one of the **list** words. Which word?

pedestrian pedal pedometer ________________

General Knowledge

1 How many sides do five triangles have altogether? ____________

2 Which day of the week takes its name from the Norse god Woden?

____

Classroom Unit 7 oo as in hoop

Your List

hoop	food	too	tool	fool	pool	boot	loot
hoot	root	moon	hoof	loop	mood	noon	soon
roof	room	doom	boom				

1 Write all of the **list** words that end with *t*.

_____________ _____________ _____________ _____________

2 Write an interesting sentence using: ***pool*** and ***boot***.

____

3 Which **list** words or **challenge** words mean…?

an animal's shoe _____________

a white bird with a yellow crest _____________

a hopping marsupial _____________

4 Write these **list** words backwards.

tool _____________ doom _____________ mood _____________

5 A **palindrome** is a word that reads the same way backwards or forwards.

Which of the **list** words is **palindromic**? _____________

6 *To*, *too* or *two*? Write the correct word in the following sentences.

The _____________ boys walked slowly _____________ the front of the classroom.

'Are you coming _____________ the playground _____________?' asked Maria.

Word Building

Strategy

All of the **list** words contain double o.

To form the **plural** (more than one) of ***roof***, add ***s***.

One roof Many r o o __ __

To form the **plural** of **hoof**, change the ***f*** to ***v*** and then add ***es***.

One hoof Many h o o __ __ __

Challenge

boomerang kangaroo cockatoo tattoo bamboo shampoo

> The wind was a torrent of darkness among the gusty trees,
> The moon was a ghostly galleon tossed upon cloudy seas.
> (Alfred Noyes)

1 Write these **list** words in dictionary order: ***moon***, ***hoop***, ***loot***, ***hoof*** and ***mood***.

____

2 Can you see **list** words hidden in these sentences?

Terry **o**rdered **o**ne **l**entil **b**urger **o**n **O**scar's **m**enu.

_ _ _ _ _ _ _ _

Rescuing **o**ld **o**striches **m**ight **n**eed **o**ur **o**blong **n**ets.

_ _ _ _ _ _ _ _

3 Which **list** words or **challenge** words mean the same as…?

stolen goods _ _ _ _ midday _ _ _ _ footwear _ _ _ _

4 Draw your favourite food, a rising moon and a swimming pool.

Word Knowledge

During a month the moon ***waxes*** and ***wanes***. One of these words means to grow bigger, while the other word means to grow smaller. Find out about these words and complete the sentences.

__________ means that the moon seems to get bigger.

__________ means that the moon seems to get smaller.

Going Going Going Gone!

General Knowledge

1 What am I? I am an Aboriginal throwing stick. Some of my kind return to the thrower.

_ _ _ _ _ _ _ _ _ _

2 What am I? I am a liquid soap. _ _ _ _ _ _ _ _

3 What am I? I am hollow grass that can grow to 10 metres in height. _ _ _ _ _ _ _

Classroom Unit **8** oo as in book

Your List

took	wood	hood	good	foot	cook	book	look
nook	rook	hook	wool	brook	stood	crook	

1 Use a dictionary to help you find the meanings of these **list** and **challenge** words.

rook ______________________________

brook ______________________________

hoodwink ______________________________

2 Write the **list** words in rhyming groups.

***ook* words**	***ood* words**	***oot* words**	***ool* words**
________	________	________	________
________	________		
________	________		
________	________		
________			
________			
________			
________			
________			

Strategy

Make word families. For example: book, look, crook and hook.

Challenge

kookaburra
hoodwink
goodbye
likelihood
woollen

3 Which **list** words or **challenge** words mean…?

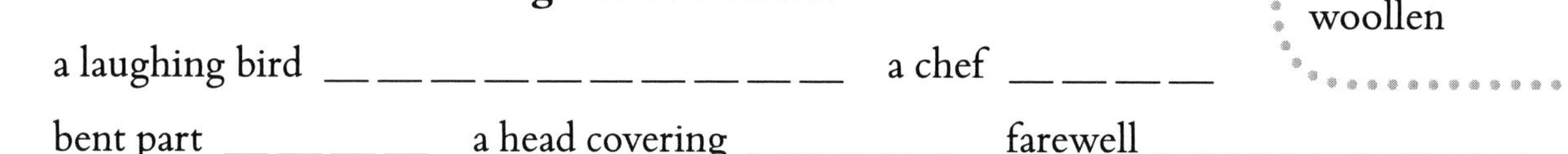

a laughing bird _ _ _ _ _ _ _ _ _ _ a chef _ _ _ _

bent part _ _ _ _ a head covering _ _ _ _ farewell _ _ _ _ _ _ _

Word Building

1 Write the **list** words that come from the words:

take _ _ _ _ stand _ _ _ _ _ feet _ _ _ _

2 Complete the following.

Something made of wood is w o o d _ _.

Someone or something wearing a hood is h o o d _ _.

Something with a crook in it is c r o o k _ _.

Home Study Unit 8

> When I look into the looking-glass
> I'm always sure to see—
> No matter, how I dodge about—Me,
> looking out at me.
>
> (C. J. Dennis)

1 Complete this Crossword, using **list** words and **challenge** words and the clues.

Across
1 a head covering
4 a laughing bird
7 to have been standing
8 a quiet corner

Down
1 curved metal
2 something at the end of your leg
3 a creek
5 something that you can read
6 to prepare a meal

2 From the **list**, draw something that you can read and something used to catch fish.

3 Add **list** words to these words to make **compound** words.

____________ball ____________work under____________

Word Knowledge

Match the following word groups with a **list** word or **challenge** word.

creek, river, stream _ _ _ _ _ _

farewell, adios, sayonara, toodle-oo _ _ _ _ _ _ _ _ _ _

view, observe, watch _ _ _ _ _

trick, deceive, fool _ _ _ _ _ _ _ _ _ _ _ _

General Knowledge

1 What do people use the following for? Merino, Corriedale, Border-Leicester ____________

2 Who was Peter Pan's main enemy? C _ _ _ _ _ _ _ _ H _ _ _

3 Balsa, teak, ply and cedar are all types of _ _ _ _ _.

Classroom Unit 9

oa as in road

Your List

oat	oak	loaf	road	roam	loan	coal	soap
boat	soak		toad	foam	moan	foal	
coat	croak		load		groan	goal	
goat							

1 Write the following words in dictionary order: ***coat***, ***load***, ***coal*** and ***loaf***.

____

2 Find the **list** words meaning:

an amphibian _ _ _ _ 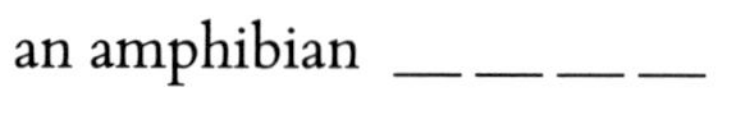   a long-living tree _ _ _   to wander _ _ _ _

a young horse _ _ _ _   you wash with this _ _ _ _   small ship _ _ _ _

3 Which **list** words are shown in these pictures?

__________ __________ __________ __________

4 Write **list** or **challenge** words that rhyme with ***wrote***.

____

5 Write **list** words that describe sounds.

__________ __________ __________

Word Building

Match the words in Group A with their partners in Group B to make new words.

Group A			Group B			New Words
row	toad	char	meal	boat	coal	__________
oat	road	coat	shooter	way	stool	__________
goal			hanger			__________
						__________
						__________
						__________
						__________

Challenge

hoax   goad   loam   bloat   loathe

The Owl and the Pussy-Cat went to sea
In a beautiful pea-green boat.
They took some honey, and plenty of money,
Wrapped up in a five-pound note.
(Edward Lear)

1 Fill in the gaps in these sentences with words from the **list**.

In the middle of the pond, on a lily-pad, sat a huge brown _ _ _ _.

After the long hike we were able to _ _ _ _ our tired feet in a bucket of hot water.

Nick was asked to buy a _ _ _ _ of bread while he was at the shop.

After our yacht sank we rowed the life- _ _ _ _ to the nearest island.

We could see the cart moving slowly along the dusty _ _ _ _.

2 Draw a toad in a coat, a goat on a road, and a foal in a boat.

Word Knowledge

Match the dictionary meanings with **challenge** words.

to tease or anger someone ____________

a trick ____________

to swell up ____________

loose fertile soil ____________

to hate ____________

General Knowledge

A young horse is called a ***foal***. What do we call the young of:

1 a goat _ _ _

2 a toad _ _ _ _ _ _ _

Classroom Unit 10 ai as in tail

Your List

ail	bail	fail	nail	jail
hail	mail	pail	rail	sail
tail	wail	trail	snail	detail

1 Write the **list** words with five or more letters in dictionary order:

____

2 Which **list** words mean…?

a bucket _ _ _ _ cry loudly _ _ _ _ prison _ _ _ _

sicken _ _ _ a shower of ice _ _ _ _ letters and parcels _ _ _ _

3 A **homophone** is a word which sounds the same as another but it is spelt differently and it has a different meaning. Write these **homophones** in sentences to show their meaning.

mail ______________________________

male ______________________________

sail ______________________________

sale ______________________________

tail ______________________________

tale ______________________________

wail ______________________________

whale ______________________________

Word Building

1 Add the endings (**suffixes**) *ing* and *ed* to these words.

fail ____________ ____________

mail ____________ ____________

sail ____________ ____________

2 Add the **suffixes** shown to form new words.

fail (ure) ____________ avail (able) ____________

Strategy

Remember that the vowels are *a e i o u*.
All the other letters are called consonants.

Challenge

daily	retail
sailor	tailor
quail	avail
available	failure
frail	thumbnail

Home Study Unit 10

Six slimy snails set sail slowly.
(Tongue Twister)

1 Draw a snail leaving a trail by a pail, and a prisoner waiting in jail.

2 Which **list** or **challenge** words would appear between the words ***frail*** and ***quail*** in a dictionary?

____________ ____________ ____________ ____________ ____________

3 Use the words from the **list** shown, to complete this Wordsearch.

L	D	A	I	L	Y	B	B	A	I	T	Q
I	P	A	I	L	T	R	A	I	L	A	U
A	H	A	I	L	S	A	I	L	O	R	A
N	F	I	A	V	A	I	L	A	I	P	I
S	R	E	T	A	I	L	L	A	I	R	L

bail	retail
hail	snail
trail	sailor
quail	daily
fail	avail
pail	

Word Knowledge

1 Add the word parts shown to make new **compound words**.

thumb + nail = ____________ rail + way = ____________

toe + nail = ____________ hail + storm = ____________

2 Is a quail a type of boat, a bird or an animal? ____________________

General Knowledge

1 Who is missing?

Tinker, _ _ _ _ _ _ _, soldier, _ _ _ _ _ _ _,

Rich man, poor man, beggar man, thief.

2 What is the name given to the reading system for blind people, which uses raised dots on the pages? ________________

ai as in rain

Your List

gain	main	pain	rain	vain	train
stain	strain	plain	grain	drain	chain
brain	again	explain	obtain	contain	complain
captain	retain	saint	faint	paint	against

1 Write these **list** words in dictionary order: ***grain***, ***stain***, ***against***, ***drain*** and ***brain***.

____

2 Which **list** words contain a smaller word that is a weather word?

__________ __________ __________ __________ __________

3 Which **list** words mean…?

ordinary _ _ _ _ _   most important _ _ _ _

to find fault _ _ _ _ _ _ _ _   suffering or hurt _ _ _ _

4 Write each of the following words in a sentence of its own to show its meaning.

rain ______________________________

rein ______________________________

reign ______________________________

plain ______________________________

plane ______________________________

pain______________________________

pane ______________________________

5 Use a dictionary to help you write a meaning for…

retain ______________________________

Word Building

Add the endings (**suffixes**) shown to form new words from the **list** and **challenge** words.

drain (age) __________________

pain (ful) __________________

main (tain) __________________

entertain (ment) __________________

Challenge

campaign	detain
entertain	abstain
ungainly	dainty
quaint	restrain

What you lose on the swings you gain on the roundabouts.
(Proverb)

1 Write, in dictionary order, all of the **list** words that begin with *c*.

____________ ____________ ____________ ____________

2 What am I? Choose answers from the **list** words.

I am the person in charge of a ship. _ _ _ _ _ _ _ _ _

I am a series of joined metal rings. _ _ _ _ _ _ _

I am what you use to think with. _ _ _ _ _ _ _

I mean suffering or hurt. _ _ _ _ _

I am a pipe or channel for carrying liquid away. _ _ _ _ _ _ _

3 Which **list** words fit into these Wordframes?

Strategy

Look at the shape of words. For example:

= gain.

Word Knowledge

Match these meanings with **challenge** words.

to control or hold back _ _ _ _ _ _ _ _ _ _ _

a long series of activities _ _ _ _ _ _ _ _ _ _ _

to keep back _ _ _ _ _ _ _ _

very delicate and pretty _ _ _ _ _ _ _ _

to stop yourself from doing something _ _ _ _ _ _ _ _ _ _

old fashioned but attractive _ _ _ _ _ _ _ _

General Knowledge

Who or what am I?

1 I am a European country. My capital is Madrid. My national sport is bull fighting.

_ _ _ _ _

2 I am a body organ. I control the way the body moves, thinks and feels. _ _ _ _ _ _

3 I am a famous river, rainforest and reef area on the north-eastern coast of Queensland. Many people have protested against my forest areas being logged.

I am the D _ _ _ _ _ _ _ _ _.

Classroom Unit 12 ea as in meat, bean, team

Your List

sea	bean	team	eat	east	beak	bead	each
tea	mean	stream	meat	beast	weak	read	reach
pea	clean	dream	seat	feast	speak		beach
flea		scream	cheat		creak		teach
			defeat				
			repeat				

Look
Say
Cover
Write
Check

1 Match these **list** words with their meanings.

defeat	where the sea meets the shore
cheat	a large meal
steam	to beat in a contest
beach	an insect
flea	water that is gas
feast	someone who is dishonest

2 Draw a circle around the correct word in brackets in these sentences.

The farmer used the (creak/creek) to pump water to his crops.

All that we could hear was the (creak/creek) of the old gate as it swung back and forth on its rusty hinges.

The girls were feeling (weak/week) and tired after running the entire length of the (beach/beech).

3 Write the **list** words which are opposites (**antonyms**) for:

untidy _ _ _ _ _   listen _ _ _ _ _ _   kind _ _ _ _

west _ _ _ _   strong _ _ _ _   learn _ _ _ _ _ _

Word Building

Match the words in Group A with the words in Group B to make new words.

Group A			Group B			New Words	
team	sea	mean	while	ball	work	________	________
beach	bean	tea	shore	eater	time	________	________
day	meat		dream	bag		________	________
						________	________

Challenge

plea	ream	gleam	preach	retreat
creature	squeak	Easter	beacon	demean

Home Study Unit 12

> Think first and speak afterwards.
> (Proverb)

1 Use **list** words to help you solve this crossword.

Across
1 not dirty
3 try to touch
4 green vegetable
5 instruct
8 group of players
9 the ocean
10 not strong

Down
1 be dishonest
2 chew
3 do again
6 squeaking noise
7 a direction

2 Which **list** words would fit into this Wordframe?
(Note: the last letter is not *t*.)

____

3 Draw a squeaking teacher, and a teatime feast of peas and beans.

Word Knowledge

1 How many words can you write that use the word *sea* as a **base word**? For example: seaside.

____

2 Which **challenge** words mean…?

a religious festival _ _ _ _ _ _ _ an animal _ _ _ _ _ _ _ _ _ _

a stack of paper _ _ _ _ _ a warning signal _ _ _ _ _ _ _ _

go backwards _ _ _ _ _ _ _ _ _ _ a request _ _ _ _ _ _

General Knowledge

1 How many players are there in each of the following sports teams? (Write numerals.)

basketball ________ soccer ________ rugby (League) ________

footy (Aussie Rules) ________ netball ________ rugby (Union) ________

2 Which beast is known as the 'King of the Jungle'? ______________

13 ow as in cow

Your List

cow	row	vow	sow	bow	brow	frown
fowl	howl	prowl	growl	scowl	crowd	drown
brown	clown	town	down	gown	crown	

1 Write all of the **list** words that contain the name of a 'wise' bird in dictionary order.

__________ __________ __________ __________ __________

2 Fill the gaps with **list** words.

We were asked to _ _ _ to the King as he walked past our group.

It was difficult to sleep with the _ _ _ coming from the children's bunkhouse.

Bernie's first job, every morning, was to feed the _ _ _ and her piglets.

The clever fox had found a way to sneak into the _ _ _ _ house without being seen.

3 Which **list** or **challenge** words mean…?

an oath __________ to sneak about __________

a comedian __________ shabby __________

jaw or cheek __________ fame __________

Strategy

Look for smaller words.
For example:
crown = crow, row, own.

4 Write down all of the words, from both lists, which have something to do with the face or head.

__________ __________ __________ __________ __________

5 Write in an interesting sentence the words: ***crown*** and ***crowd***.

____

Word Building

Match the words in Group A with the words in Group B to form **compound words**.
(A **compound word** is one word made up of two different words.)

Group A			Group B			Compound Words
town	down	how	ever	how	fall	__________
any	town	down	ship	pour	house	__________
						__________
						__________
						__________

Challenge

dowdy renown jowl towel cowl

> James James said to his Mother,
> 'Mother,' he said, said he;
> 'You must never go down to the end of the town if you don't go down with me.'
>
> (A. A. Milne)

1 Draw a scowling clown and a frowning cow.

Draw a brown owl bowing before a growling king with a crown covering his brow.

2 Is a cowl a bird, a male cow or a hood? ______________________________

Word Knowledge

Write five **list** words to which ***ing*** can be added.

____

General Knowledge

1 Where are the Crown Jewels kept? The Tower of London? The Tower of Babel? The Charters Towers Civic Centre? ____________________

2 A sow is a female pig. What is a male pig called? _ _ _ _

3 Which Australian Prime Minister is supposed to have drowned at Cheviot Beach in Victoria in 1967? ____________________

Classroom Unit 14 ear as in near

Your List

ear	near	year	tear	gear	hear
dear	rear	fear	clear	spear	appear
shear	beard	smear			

1 **Homophones** are words which sound the same but have different meanings and they are spelt differently, for example: ***hear*** means to be able to sense sounds, while ***here*** means in this place.
Write the correct word from the brackets in the gaps in these sentences.

(hear/here) I could ____________ the rustling of leaves as the wombat waddled nearer.

(hear/here) 'There is plenty of room for you to park over ____________!' called the attendant.

(dear/deer) The ____________ grazed peacefully, unaware of the approaching lion.

(shear/sheer) The farmers believed it would be a ____________ waste of time to ____________ the flock too early.

(dear/deer) 'Children's toys are so ____________!' complained the customer.

2 **Homographs** are words which sound the same and have the same spelling but they have different meanings, for example: 'dear' means someone or something special, and it also means something expensive. Use the following **homographs** in the gaps in the sentences below: ***dear***, ***rear*** and ***gear***.

The present was far too ____________, even to buy for my ____________ friend Tasha.

The children were allowed to ____________ the chickens in a coop at the ____________ of the shed.

The driver couldn't move the important scientific ____________ because the ____________ lever in the truck had snapped off.

Word Building

Add the **suffixes** shown in brackets to form new words from these **list** words.

fear (ful) ________________

fear (less) ________________

fear (some) ________________

dear (est) ________________

year (ly) ________________

near (ly) ________________

clear (ance) ________________

tear (ful) ________________

Challenge

dreary endear earwig sear nearly nuclear

Home Study Unit 14

> Fools rush in where angels fear to tread.
> (Proverb)

1 Which **list** or **challenge** words mean…?

hair growing on the face ____________

hearing organ ____________

dull or depressing ____________

a weapon ____________

to scorch ____________

365 days ____________

2 Write an interesting sentence using the words: ***fear***, ***year*** and ***nearly***.

____

3 Write **list** words for each of these pictures.

____________ ____________ ____________

4 Write the **list** words or **challenge** words that best fit the gaps in these sentences.

The family spent the _ _ _ _ _ _ _ _ winter afternoon huddled around the fire.

Lily's habit was to _ _ _ _ _ _ Vegemite all over her toast.

We watched as one bird after another began to _ _ _ _ _ _ _ _ on the park bench.

5 Write words from the **list** that are the opposites (**antonyms**) for the following:

disappear ____________ far ____________ cheap ____________

Word Knowledge

From which **list** words do these words come?

shorn ____________

clarity ____________

apparent ____________

hearsay ____________

General Knowledge

1 When will the next leap year be? ____________

2 Who am I? I am famous for my nonsense poems. One of my poems was about an owl and a pussy-cat.

E _ _ _ _ _ _ L _ _ _

3 If you suffer from arachnophobia what do you fear? ____________

15 aw as in jaw

Your List

jaw	law	raw	paw	gnaw	straw	
draw	claw	thaw	flaw	crawl	sprawl	scrawl
bawl	brawl	shawl	trawl			
dawn	lawn	yawn	fawn			
hawk	gawk		awful		drawers	

1 Write the **list** words that have five letters in dictionary order.

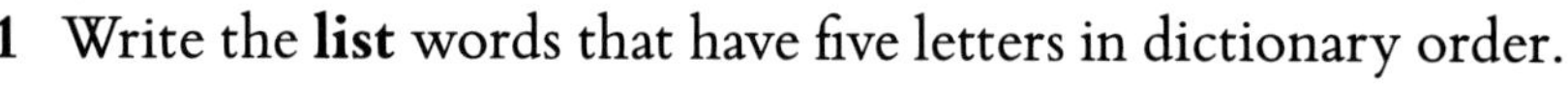

____

2 Write an interesting sentence using the words: ***lawn***, ***crawl*** and ***dawn***.

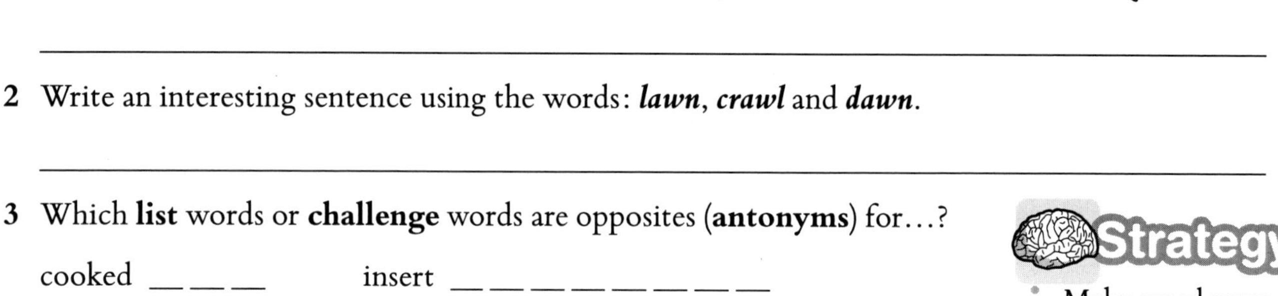

____

3 Which **list** words or **challenge** words are opposites (**antonyms**) for…?

cooked _ _ _ insert _ _ _ _ _ _ _ _

freeze _ _ _ _ dusk _ _ _ _

Strategy

Make word sums.
For example:
dr + aw = draw
tr + awl = trawl.

4 Write the **list** words which best fit the gaps in these sentences.

It is the job of the police to uphold the _ _ _.

After a wide _ _ _ _ the princess fell asleep on the bed of golden _ _ _ _ _.

The suburbs of large cities _ _ _ _ _ _ _ out in many directions.

The children folded their clothes and put them neatly in their _ _ _ _ _ _ _.

5 Can you find the **list** words or **challenge** words hidden in these sentences?

Young **a**nimals **w**alk **n**imbly. _ _ _ _

Before **r**unning, **a**lways **w**alk **l**ightly. _ _ _ _ _

Word Building

A **compound word** is made up of two other words. Write the **list** words and **challenge** words in these **compound words**.

jawbone ____________ withdraw ____________

strawberry ____________ lawnmower ____________

backcrawl ____________ law-abiding ____________

Challenge

awkward chainsaw dawdle hacksaw lawyer strawberry tawny withdraw

It is the last straw that breaks the camel's back.
(Proverb)

1 Which **list** words would fit into these Wordframes?

2 Draw a fawn and a hawk see-sawing on a lawn.

3 Write meanings for these **list** words. A dictionary may help.

gnaw ______________________________

shawl ______________________________

flaw ______________________________

Word Knowledge

A trawler is a type of fishing boat. Can you explain why it might be called a trawler?

____

____

General Knowledge

1 I am the name given to the young of a deer. ______________

2 Who am I? I was a famous Australian writer. I wrote such stories as 'The Loaded Dog' and 'The Drover's Wife'.

H _ _ _ _ L _ _ _ _ _ _

3 Who am I? I was an Antarctic explorer. My name is used for one of Australia's Antarctic bases.

D _ _ _ _ _ _ _ _ M _ _ _ _ _ _

Classroom Unit 16 igh as in sigh; ight as in night

Your List

high	sigh	thigh	nigh	all right	plight	highlight	fortnight
night	light	tight	right	might	sight	fight	lightning
fright	knight	bright	flight	slight	delight	midnight	twilight

1 **Homophones** are words which sound the same as others but which have different meanings and different spellings. Write each of these **homophones** in a sentence.

right ______

write ______

knight ______

night ______

sight ______

site ______

2 Write these words in dictionary order: ***high***, ***sigh***, ***nigh***, ***thigh***, ***fight*** and ***light***.

______ ______ ______

______ ______ ______

3 The word ***light*** is a **homograph**. Write two meanings of ***light***.

______

______

Word Building

1 Add ***ing*** to the following words.

fight ______ sight ______

delight ______ light ______

2 Add ***en*** and then add ***ing*** to these words.

bright ______ fright ______

tight ______ light ______

Choose two of the eight new words you have just written to fill in the gaps in this sentence.

The first ______ of the terrible dragon had been the most ______ for us.

Strategy

Make word sums.
For example:
l + ight = light
br + ight = bright.

Challenge

alight bight
blight insight
limelight nightingale

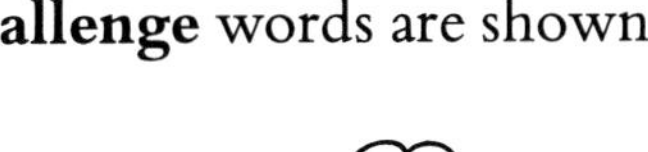

Red sky at night shepherd's delight, red sky in the morning shepherd take warning.

(Proverb)

1 Which **list** and **challenge** words are shown in these pictures?

_____________ _____________ _____________ _____________

2 Write the **list** words that would come between ***bright*** and ***plight*** in a dictionary.

_____________ _____________ _____________ _____________ _____________

_____________ _____________ _____________ _____________ _____________

_____________ _____________ _____________ _____________

3 Which **list** or **challenge** words mean…?

the dim light before sunset _ _ _ _ _ _ _ _ _ _ _

a bend or curve in the shoreline _ _ _ _ _ _ _

upper leg _ _ _ _ _ _ twelve o'clock at night _ _ _ _ _ _ _ _ _ _

4 True or False?

We usually delight in breakfast at midnight. _____________

It is not usually light at night. _____________ A knight enjoys flight. _____________

One would enjoy the plight of being struck by lightning. _____________

Word Knowledge

Write the words ***lightning*** and ***lightening*** in separate sentences, showing their meanings.

____

____

General Knowledge

1 Who am I? I was an early Governor of New South Wales. I was the captain of the ship *Bounty* when my crew mutinied against me.

I am W _ _ _ _ _ _ _ _ B _ _ _ _ _

2 What do the following people have in common?
Sir Donald Bradman Sir Bob Geldof Sir Robert Menzies Sir Lancelot

____

The magic e and vowel sounds

Your List

tame	zone	green	school	hook	float	cone	need
	coop	wood	fake	tone	room	crawl	
	fright	frail	appear	explain	scream	growl	

1 Write in dictionary order all of the **list** words that end with ***e***.

____

2 Which **list** words rhyme with…?

fool _ _ _ _ _ _ complain _ _ _ _ _ _ _

dream _ _ _ _ _ _ brawl _ _ _ _ _

fear _ _ _ _ _ _ stake _ _ _ _

3 Write an interesting sentence using the words: ***school***, ***zone*** and ***need***.

____

____

4 Which **list** words mean…?

weak _ _ _ _ _ a small cage for hens or pigeons _ _ _ _

not wild _ _ _ _ not real _ _ _ _

a musical sound _ _ _ _ a special area _ _ _ _

a colour _ _ _ _ _ shout loudly _ _ _ _ _ _

5 Which **list** words are the opposites (**antonyms**) of…?

sink _ _ _ _ _ wild _ _ _ _ strong _ _ _ _ _

Strategy

Look at the shape of words.
For example:
green = 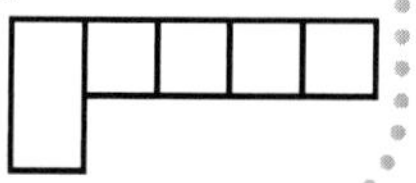

Word Building

Add ***ing***, ***er***, ***ed*** or ***est*** to the following to make new words.

tame ________ ________ ________ ________

scream ________ ________ ________

fake ________ ________ ________

green ________ ________

explain ________ ________

need ________ ________

frail ________ ________

Challenge

coax	drawl
investigate	eyesight
spool	suppose

A friend in need is a friend indeed.
(Proverb)

Classroom Review 1

1 Use this code to find the **list** words.

a	b	c	d	e	f	g	h	i	j	k	l	m	n	o	p	q	r	s	t	u	v	w	x	y	z
z	y	x	w	v	u	t	s	r	q	p	o	n	m	l	k	j	i	h	g	f	e	d	c	b	a

x i z d o = _ _ _ _ _ x l m v = _ _ _ _ h x i v z n = _ _ _ _ _ _

u o l z g = _ _ _ _ _ x l l k = _ _ _ _ z k k v z i = _ _ _ _ _ _

2 Write the **list** words which have:

a magic *e* ______ ______ ______ ______ ______

a double **vowel** sound (for example, *oo*, *ee*) ______ ______

______ ______ ______ ______ ______

a combined **vowel** sound (for example, *ea*, *oa*) ______ ______

______ ______ ______

a **vowel** and a **consonant** sound (for example, *ow*) ______ ______

3 Draw something that might give you a fright if it were to appear in the room.

Word Knowledge

Match the **challenge** words with their meanings.

to take as being fact _ _ _ _ _ _ _ _ _ the power of seeing _ _ _ _ _ _ _ _ _ _

to speak slowly _ _ _ _ _ _ to look at closely _ _ _ _ _ _ _ _ _ _ _ _ _ _ _ _ _

to persuade gently _ _ _ _ _ a cylinder for tape, string, wool etc. _ _ _ _ _ _ _

General Knowledge

1 Which of the following shapes is a cone?

   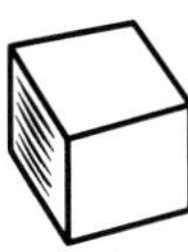

2 What is the usual speed limit for vehicles in a school zone during school hours? ______

Classroom Unit 17 ch as in chin; th as in they

Your List

chin	char	chess	the	those	than
chop	chest	chance	they	these	them
chew	chill	cherry	then	there	that
chip	chat	chalk	this	their	though

1 Which **list** or **challenge** words mean...?

burn to charcoal _ _ _ _ a small church _ _ _ _ _ _

a fruit _ _ _ _ _ _ a tool _ _ _ _ _ _

a board game _ _ _ _ _ coldness _ _ _ _ _

2 True or False?

You chew chocolate with a chisel. __________

You might find charcoal in a chimney. __________

Winter is a time for chats about chills in the chest. __________

3 Which **list** words fit best into these gaps...?

now and __________ here and __________

this and __________ these and __________

4 Write the smaller words in these **list** words. For example: those = hose.

chill = _ _ _ _ chisel = _ _ _ chocolate = _ _ _ _ chat = _ _ _

Word Building

1 To add ***ed*** or ***ing*** to the following words, you must double the last letter.

chop _ _ _ _ _ _ _ _ _ _ _ _ _ _ _ _

chip _ _ _ _ _ _ _ _ _ _ _ _ _ _ _ _

chat _ _ _ _ _ _ _ _ _ _ _ _ _ _ _ _

2 New words can also be formed by adding words to ***there***. Complete the following.

there + fore = __________ there + by = __________

there + upon = __________

Finish the following sentence by adding an ending of your own.

The train arrived early therefore __________

Challenge

chapel	charcoal
chimney	chisel
chocolate	therefore
themselves	challenge
champion	chief

17

Where there's a will there's a way.
(Proverb)

1 Write in dictionary order the words: ***chin***, ***chat***, ***chew***, ***chop*** and ***chip***.

____

2 Which list words fit into these Wordframes?

3 Draw a chess piece, a sharp chisel, a tall chimney and a ripe cherry.

4 ***Their*** means belonging to them. ***There*** means in that place. ***They're*** is short for they are.
Fill in the gaps in these sentences with the correct word.

The children collected ____________ books and moved to a new classroom.

Lions can be dangerous in the wild because ____________ man-eaters.

'We will meet over ____________, by the main gate,' called the teacher.

Word Knowledge

1 Change the following words to more than one (**plural**). The clues in brackets may help you.

chest (add *s*) ________________ cherry (*y* to *i*, add *es*) ________________

chimney (add *s*) ________________ chance (add *s*) ________________

2 Write one sentence with as many of the ***th*** words as possible.
Remember that the sentence must make sense.

____

General Knowledge

1 Name three countries which begin with 'Ch'.
Ch ________________ Ch ________________ Ch ________________

2 What am I? I am the swiftest of all cats. _ _ _ _ _ _ _

3 I was originally known by the Aztecs as *Xocolat*, the 'drink of the gods' but today I am known as _ _ _ _ _ _ _ _ _.

Classroom Unit 18 bl- pl- sl- cl- gl- fl-

Your List

blot	plot	slot	clap	glad	fly
blow	play	slap	club	glow	flat
blur	plan	slim	clay	glum	flag
blast	plug	slip	clash	glove	flash
blush	plenty	slow	clever	glory	flesh

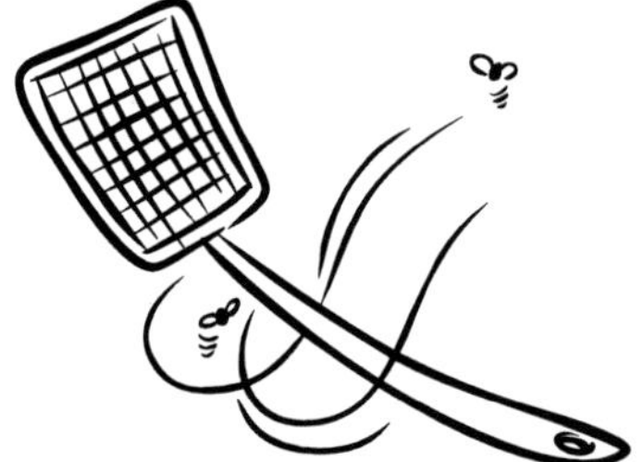

1 Write all of the **list** words that begin with *cl* in dictionary order.

____

2 Match these meanings with **list** words.

go red in the face _ _ _ _ _   unhappy _ _ _ _   a design _ _ _ _

lots _ _ _ _ _ _   dense earth _ _ _ _   a small piece of ground _ _ _ _

a hand covering _ _ _ _ _

3 Use **list** words to complete these sentences.

After the loud _ _ _ _ of thunder a bright _ _ _ _ _ of lightning lit up the sky.

The _ _ _ _ _ _ fox was able to _ _ _ _ through the trap.

Word Building

Add *ed* and *ing* to the following words. IMPORTANT: If there is a short **vowel** (a e i o u) before the last letter, then you must double the last letter before adding the ending. For example: plan = *planned* and *planning*.

blot	________	________	plot	________	________
slot	________	________	blast	________	________
blush	________	________	flash	________	________
slip	________	________	slim	________	________
club	________	________	blur	________	________
slap	________	________	glow	________	________

Challenge

clergy   clumsy   flamingo   flimsy   florist
glacier   planet   platypus   pluck   slouch

Home Study Unit 18

> It's an ill wind that blows nobody any good.
> (Proverb)

1 Complete this Wordsearch using only the **list** words beginning with ***fl*** and ***pl***.

O	F	P	L	L	F	E	P
F	P	L	O	T	L	Y	L
L	F	L	A	O	A	A	E
A	P	L	U	G	T	L	N
S	T	Y	A	Y	A	P	T
H	L	F	L	E	S	H	Y
F	D	P	L	A	N	Y	A

2 Which **list** words are shown here?

________________ ________________ ________________

3 Which **list** words mean…?

an explosion _ _ _ _ _ _ intelligent and skilful _ _ _ _ _ _ _ _ skin _ _ _ _ _ _

shine in the dark _ _ _ _ _ something unclear _ _ _ _ _ a stain _ _ _ _ _

4 Which **list** words rhyme with…?

some __________ grey __________ __________ her __________

Word Knowledge

Use a dictionary to help you find which **challenge** word:

is a large mass of ice ________________

comes from the name Flora, the goddess of flowers ________________

comes from the Latin word *clericus* and means priests or ministers of Christian churches

____

General Knowledge

1 There are only two monotremes in the world. The echidna is one, what is the other?

____

2 Name the eight official planets of the solar system.

____

3 Who wrote the poem *Clancy of the Overflow*? ________________________

Classroom Unit 19 sm- sn- sw- sk- st- sp- sh-

Your List

smog	snap	swim	ski	stop	spot	ship
small	snip	swan	sky	step	spin	show
smell	snag	sway	skin	stew	spell	shut
smack	snug	swing	skull	stay	spider	shell
	snow		skill	story		shock
	snack			still		
				stick		

Make word sums. For example:
sk + in = skin
sm + ack = smack.

1 Write the **list** words beginning with ***sm*** in dictionary order.

__________ __________ __________ __________

2 Which **list** words mean the same as these (**synonyms**)?

odour __________ close __________ break __________

hit __________ halt __________ pace __________

3 Use the code A = 1, B = 2, C = 3 etc. to find these **list** words:
For example: 19 14 21 7 = snug.

19 16 5 12 12 _ _ _ _ _ 19 23 1 25 _ _ _ _

19 13 1 12 12 _ _ _ _ _ 19 8 15 3 11 _ _ _ _ _

4 Which **list** words mean…?

pollution __________ food cooked slowly __________

to display __________ frozen rain drops __________

a long-necked bird __________ a snail's home __________

Word Building

1 Add ***ed*** and ***ing*** to the following words. (Don't forget you may need to double the last letter.)

shock __________ __________ spot __________ __________

stay __________ __________ snap __________ __________

2 Which **list** words can be added to the following words to make **compound words**?
(A **compound word** is one word made from two other words. Example: football)

_ _ _ _ shot _ _ _ _ _ shape _ _ _ lift shell _ _ _ _ _

Challenge

shadow shallow shovel skeleton smuggler spaghetti
spirit stir stomach storey studio swerve

Home Study Unit 19

> No stir in the air, no stir in the sea,
> The ship was as still as she could be.
> (Robert Southey)

1 Draw a star on a stork stuck in a stew.

2 Which **list** words mean…?

the bone in which the brain rests _ _ _ _ _

twist quickly _ _ _ _ a tale _ _ _ _ _

not moving _ _ _ _ _ little _ _ _ _ _

move through water _ _ _ _

3 Which **list** words are shown in these pictures?

______ ______ ______

Word History

Spaghetti is an Italian word that means little cords.
Can you think of more food words that come from other languages?

Word Knowledge

1 Who is more likely to carry out skullduggery—a smuggler or a skeleton?

______

2 Write the words ***story*** and ***storey*** in separate sentences to show their meanings.

______

______

3 Can a stomach hold spaghetti? ______

Can a spider spin? ______

Is it usual to use a shovel in a studio? ______

General Knowledge

1 The following are major Australian sports stadiums. In which city is each located?

M.C.G. ______ S.C.G. ______

W.A.C.A ______ Gabba ______

2 In which country do Shinto priests bless dolls of children during Hino Matsuri?

______

3 At what time during daylight hours is your shadow likely to be smallest? ______

Classroom Unit 20 cr– gr– tr– br– dr– pr– fr– wr-

Your List

crab	grin	trot	brim	drum	pray	frog	wrong
crowd	grab	trip	bring	drop	prey	frost	wrap
crown	grey	trap	brush	draw	prowl	Friday	written
crew	grip		branch		problem		
crash					prison		

1 Write **list** words in the gaps in these sentences.

We watched the cat ______ quietly across the rooftops.

After a search of the ______ site the rescuers found all of the _____ safe and well.

People who are on the ______ side of the law often end up in _______.

'After you have ________ out the words, you can _____ a picture for each one,' instructed Ms Bennett.

2 Which **list** words mean…?

an amphibian ____ a seashore creature ____ a colour ____

a tree's limb ______ a week day ______ a journey ____

3 ***Pray*** and ***prey*** are **homophones** (words which sound the same but have different spellings and different meanings). Write each **homophone** in a sentence.

____

____

4 Write the words from the **list** and **challenge** boxes beginning with a silent letter in dictionary order. _____ _____ _____ _____

Word Building

Add ***ed*** and ***ing*** to the following words. (Don't forget that you may need to double the last letter.)

trap	_____	_____	prowl	_____	_____
drop	_____	_____	crowd	_____	_____
grin	_____	_____	brim	_____	_____
grab	_____	_____	drum	_____	_____

Challenge

brother	brown	crayon	crimson	drama	friend	graph	grocer
prepare	product	proper	travel	trial	trust	wren	

Home Study Unit 20

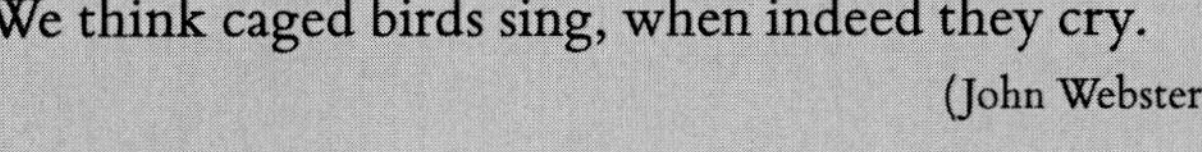

We think caged birds sing, when indeed they cry.
(John Webster)

1 Find the **list** words shown below in this Wordsearch.

A	S	C	C	T	D	R	U	M	S
P	R	R	S	R	G	R	A	B	N
T	R	O	T	V	A	B	R	I	M
A	R	W	R	A	P	S	R	N	C
F	O	D	R	O	P	G	H	U	T

brim	frost
crash	grab
crowd	grin
drop	trot
drum	wrap

Word History
In Norse (Viking) history Frigg was the wife of the god Odin. Which day of the week do you think was celebrated as Frigg's Day?

2 Which **list** words are opposites (**antonyms**) for the following…?

hunter ____________ right ____________ solution ____________

3 Which **list** words best fit into the following groups?

shell starfish jellyfish ____________ creep crawl sneak ____________

smile smirk beam ____________ grasp hold snatch ____________

limb bough twig ____________ canter gallop prance ____________

Word Knowledge

Tri means three. Use a dictionary to help you write the meanings of these words:

triangle ____________ tricycle ____________

tricep ____________ trident ____________

tricolour ____________ tripod ____________

trilogy ____________ tricorne ____________

General Knowledge

1 What are the three events of the triathlon? ____________ ____________ ____________

2 The Superb Blue, Fairy and Splendid are all types of which bird? ____________

3 What am I? I am Western Australia's second largest city. _ _ _ _ _ _ _ _ _ _ _

Classroom Unit 21 –ng –nd –nt –nk

Your List

sing	bang	ring	king	long	wing	hang	fang
land	sand	stand	band	send	bend	spend	second
mind	find	kind	grind	blind	sent	cent	scent
went	tent	want	front	print	plant	grunt	giant
tank	bank	blank	thank	plank	pink	think	trunk

1 Which **list** words mean…?

crush up ________________ use money ________________

a long tooth ________________ discover ________________

a colour ________________ use your mind ________________

2 Write in dictionary order: ***sing***, ***wing***, ***king***, ***pink***, ***find*** and ***kind***.

____

3 Write an interesting sentence that includes any three **list** words.

____

4 Which **list** words rhyme with ***blind***?

____________ ____________ ____________ ____________

5 Write all of the **list** words which have a smaller word in them which means finish.

____________ ____________ ____________

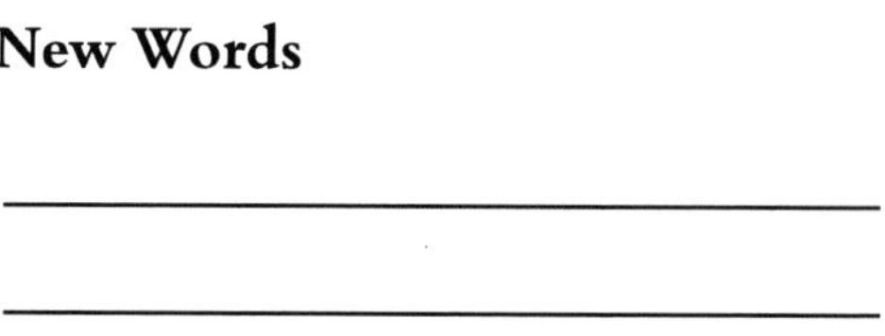

Word Building

Join the words in Box A with the words in Box B to form new **compound words**. (Words can be used more than once.)

A

band	under	land
quick	grand	hand
over	thank	news

B

sand	shake	stand
hang	you	print
mark	slide	

New Words

____

____

____

____

____

____

Challenge

billabong	ailment	prolong	descend
among	reprimand	excellent	elephant

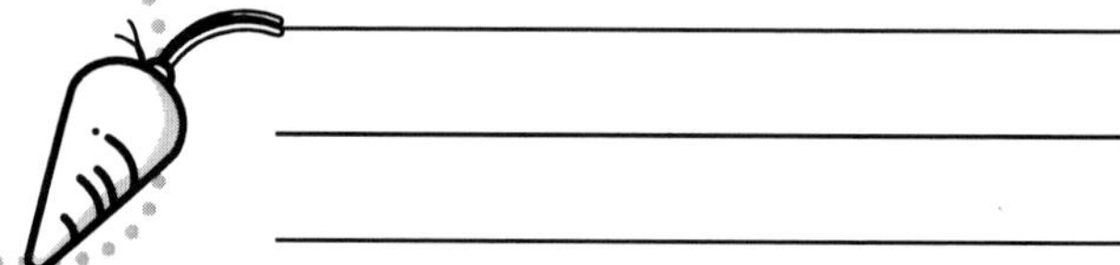

Home Study Unit 21

> There's none so blind as those who will not see.
> (Proverb)

1 Use the beginnings on the left and the endings in the box to make as many **list** words as you can.

s–	w–	*ing*
k–	th–	*ind*
m–	gr–	*ink*
r–	bl–	

____

____

____

____

2 Finish this crossword using the clues and the **list** words.

Across
1 make musical sounds with the voice
3 circle
5 container for liquid
7 canvas home

Down
1 fragrance
2 pig-like noise
4 huge person
6 ruler

3 Which **list** words would fit in this Wordframe?

______________ ______________ ______________

4 Which **list** words are opposites (**antonyms**) for…?

short _ _ _ _   sit _ _ _ _ _   save _ _ _ _ _   lose _ _ _ _

Word Knowledge

Which **challenge** words would be the best 'partners' for these words?

a mountain ______________   a trunk ______________

a bunyip ______________   medicine ______________

General Knowledge

1 To which 'lands' do the following belong?

Big Ben, Stonehenge, the River Thames, _ _ _ land

clogs, tulips, windmills, dykes, _ _ _ land

shamrock, St Patrick, leprechauns, _ _ _ land

Siam, baht, Bangkok, monsoon, _ _ _ _ land

2 What am I? I am the largest living land mammal. ______________

3 What am I? I am a smooth-scaled lizard. s _ _ _ k

Classroom Unit 22 -st -sh

Your List

most	lost	past	mist	rust	nest	first
post	cost	last	fist	dust	test	worst
almost	fast	exist	must	west	burst	cash
rush	forest	dish	fresh	finish	wash	push
bush	wish	suggest	varnish	fish	contest	interest

Look
Say
Cover
Write
Check

1 Which **list** words mean…?

clean with water ____________ a bird's home ____________

new ______________ closed hand ______________

end ______________ final ______________

2 Which **list** words rhyme with…?

toast ____________ ____________ tossed ____________

missed ____________ ____________ ____________ posh ____________

3 Write **list** words in the gaps in these sentences.

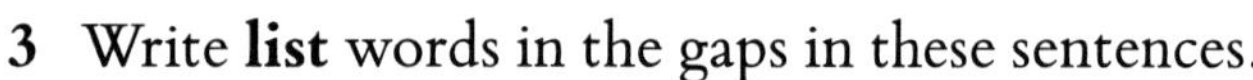

Even though we walked w __ __ __ through the f __ __ __ __ __ we still became l __ __ __.

As the runner crossed the f __ __ __ __ __ line she held up a clenched f __ __ __.

4 Finish these word groups by adding a **list** word.

jungle, woods ______________________ scrub, rinse, scour ______________

cheques, coins, credit cards ______________ exam, trial ______________

Word Building

Add the word part shown in brackets to form new words.

(dis) + honest ____________________ punish + (ment) ____________________

suggest + (ion) ____________________ astonish + (ment) ____________________

(dis) + interest ____________________ exist + (ence) ____________________

post + (age) ____________________ fast + (en) ____________________

Challenge

dentist	enlist	guest	harvest	honest
astonish	harsh	punish	rubbish	selfish

> It is the first step that is the most difficult.
> (Proverb)

1 Write these **list** words in dictionary order: ***last***, ***post***, ***fist***, ***test*** and ***wish***.

____

2 Which **list** word am I?

I am a hand that is closed tightly. ______________

I am before second. ______________

I am what happens to tin when left in the rain. ______________

I am a common name for the Australian countryside. ______________

3 Which **list** words do you think of when you look at these pictures?

______________ ______________ ______________

4 Find the **list** words ending with **sh** in this Wordsearch.

C	P	E	R	R	U	S	H
A	F	W	V	U	D	F	D
S	C	I	A	S	M	I	I
H	A	H	S	S	E	N	S
F	R	E	S	H	H	I	H
W	I	S	H	C	N	S	A
J	O	S	M	R	E	H	V
W	U	K	P	U	S	H	G
B	V	A	R	N	I	S	H

Word Knowledge

Which **challenge** words mean…?

junk ______________ picking crops ______________

amaze ______________ hard ______________

a person who cares for teeth ______________

thinking of only one's self ______________ a visitor at one's home ______________

General Knowledge

1 What do the following all have in common? trout, redfin, flathead and flounder

____

2 What languages are spoken in these countries?

Sweden ____________ Turkey ____________ Denmark ____________ Spain ____________

3 What is the Olympic contest that is a foot race of 42 kilometres? ______________

Classroom Unit 23 –ck

Your List

rock	lock	dock	knock	block	clock	
sick	pick	kick	brick	quick		
luck	duck	truck	pluck	peck	neck	deck
rack	back	sack	track	crack	black	attack

1 Write the **list** words ending with ***ock*** in dictionary order.

____

____

2 Which **list** words mean…?

jab with beak ____________ ship's platform ____________

water bird ____________ frame for storing things ____________

select ____________ body part between head and shoulders ____________

3 ***Pick*** is a **homograph** and so is ***rock***. A **homograph** is a word which has more than one meaning even though the spelling doesn't change.
Use ***pick*** or ***rock*** in the gaps in these sentences.

If you do not ________ the correct box you will not win the prize.

The worker used a ________ to break up the ________.

Dad would always ________ the cradle back and forth to put our baby sister to sleep.

4 Which **list** words are **antonyms** (opposites) for these…?

slow _ _ _ _ _ front _ _ _ _ white _ _ _ _ _

retreat _ _ _ _ _ _ well _ _ _ _ unblock _ _ _ _ _

Word Building

Form **compound words** by joining groups from the two groups below.
(Words may be used more than once.)

Group A	Group B			New Words
back	bone	pack	ward	____________
crack	pot	suit	ground	____________
black	down	track	out	____________
track	hand	door		____________
				____________
				____________

Challenge

limerick
shipwreck
ransack
livestock
candlestick
dumbstruck

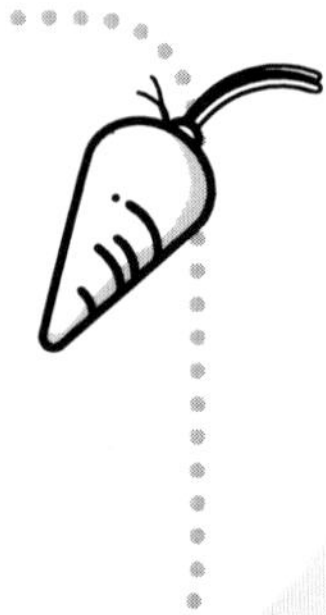

Home Study Unit 23

The worse luck now, the better another time.
(Proverb)

1 Find all of the five-lettered **list** words in this Wordsearch.

W	B	L	A	C	K	K	G	C	K	Q
O	L	H	V	P	N	M	O	C	K	U
C	O	K	C	L	O	C	K	C	N	I
K	C	B	D	U	C	U	A	L	K	C
A	K	G	R	C	K	R	F	C	O	K
V	H	D	K	K	C	A	I	O	L	K
C	S	M	O	W	T	R	A	C	K	H
T	R	U	C	K	B	C	T	C	K	E

2 Which **list** words could match these jobs or hobbies?

builder ____________ gardener ____________ wharfie ____________

watchmaker ____________ bushwalker ____________ Santa Claus ____________

sailor ____________ nurse ____________ footballer ____________

truckie ____________ soldier ____________ locksmith ____________

3 Which **list** words (in order) would come between ***peck*** and ***truck*** in a dictionary?

____

____

4 Write a sentence containing one of the **challenge** words.

____

Word Knowledge

Find an example of a limerick or a knock-knock joke and write it on a separate piece of paper or card.

(You could make up your own if you wish.)

General Knowledge

1 Who am I? I am a fairytale character. I traded my mother's cow for some beans.

____

2 Who am I? I am a member of a famous band of outlaws. I lived in Sherwood Forest with Robin Hood. I was a religious member of the band.

I am F _ _ _ _ T _ _ _

3 How do we describe the sound made by a duck? ____________

Classroom Unit 24 –th

Your List

path	bath	myth	cloth	north	filth	growth		
depth	length	teeth	tooth					
fourth	fifth	sixth	seventh	eighth	ninth	tenth	eleventh	twelfth

Strategy

Look for smaller words.
For example:
tenth = ten tent
forth = or for fort.

1 Which **list** words…?

have three **vowels** ____________________

have two **vowels** ____________________

have no **vowels** ____________________

2 Write as words.

5th __________ 8th __________ 6th __________

12th __________ 4th __________ 9th __________

11th __________ 10th __________ 7th __________

3 Which **list** words mean…?

legend __________ how deep __________ distance along __________

a direction __________ something disgustingly dirty __________

4 Use **list** or **challenge** words to fill the gaps in these sentences.

We walked along the gravel __________ until we had covered its entire __________.

It took a long soapy __________ to wash off the __________ from the mudfight.

The teacher read the __________ about a quest for a dragon with golden __________.

5 Which **list** words have been formed from these words?

grow __________ long __________ deep __________

Word Building

Match the words in Group A with the words in Group B to form **compound words**.

Group A		Group B		New Words
path	bath	ache	cloth	__________
dish	tooth	room	way	__________
				__________
				__________

Challenge

hearth girth
pith mirth
sleuth

Don't throw the baby out with the bath water.
(Proverb)

1 An **acrostic** poem is one in which the first letter of each line spells a word.
For example:

Monsters, dragons and mysteries
Yetis and yowies
Terrifying tales of
Horrible beasts.

Select a word from your **list** and write an **acrostic** poem.

____
____
____
____
____
____

2 Which **list** words would fit into this Wordframe?

__________ __________ __________

3 Which **list** words fit here?

f __ f __ h   __ l __ __ e __ __ h   __ or __ __

Word Knowledge

1 Which **list** words match the following…?

mythological __________   bathe __________

2 Match these dictionary meanings with **challenge** words.

amusement and laughter __________

the measurement around anything __________

the floor of a fireplace __________

spongy middle of a plant, stem, fruit etc. __________

a detective or investigator __________

HA HA HA

General Knowledge

1 What am I? I am a slow-moving, tree-dwelling mammal from South and Central America.

__ __ __ __ __

2 Which magical and mythical creature is supposed to replace children's lost teeth with money?

____

3 Which direction is opposite to north? __________

Consonant blends/Beginnings and endings

Your List

child	their	block	slack	fling
chicken	there	pluck	click	gloom
stock	stuck	shock	list	worth
crush	prong	tram	brink	mend

Strategy

Look for smaller words.
For example:
block = lock
brink = in ink.

1 Use **list** words to fill the gaps in these sentences.

The ducks fluffed _ _ _ _ _ feathers to keep themselves warm.

'We can sit over _ _ _ _ _, under that gum tree, for lunch,' announced Dad.

'How much is this toy car _ _ _ _ _?' Bert asked the shopkeeper.

To help them remember their shopping, Anna and Carl wrote a long _ _ _ _.

The small, lost _ _ _ _ _ cried in the _ _ _ _ _ of the football crowd.

2 Which **list** words mean…?

the edge ____________ a young hen ____________

throw ____________ repair ____________

a passenger vehicle ____________ a spike ____________

3 Which **list** words contain these smaller words?

rush ____________ end ____________ ram ____________

Word Building

1 Add the endings and beginnings shown in the brackets to make new words.

worth (less) ____________ child (ren) ____________

stock (ade) ____________ shock (wave) ____________

(black) list ____________ there (abouts) ____________

2 Add *ing* to the following words.

stock ____________ shock ____________

list ____________ crush ____________

gnash ____________ pluck ____________

Challenge

wealth church
wrath gnash

> The worth of a thing is what it will bring.
> (Proverb)

1 Find the **list** words shown in this Wordsearch.

block	fling
brink	gloom
chicken	list
child	mend
click	stock
crush	their

A	H	L	I	S	T	O	P	L	A	E	D
S	T	O	C	K	B	R	I	N	K	C	L
A	B	K	C	L	O	F	T	U	V	E	G
C	A	L	O	C	H	I	C	K	E	N	L
H	E	C	O	T	H	E	I	R	I	U	O
I	H	Y	E	C	L	S	U	L	M	E	O
L	C	L	I	C	K	R	F	O	E	J	M
D	F	R	U	T	C	F	K	U	N	O	C
E	C	L	C	R	U	S	H	I	D	L	H

2 Write **list** words for each of these pictures.

____________ ____________ ____________

Word History

Some sound words are spelt the way they sound.
For example: ***click***.
Can you think of any other words that make the sound you are describing when you say them?

3 Which **list** words fit into these Wordframes?

Use a dictionary to find the meanings of these **challenge** words.

wealth ________________________

wrath ________________________

gnash ________________________

General Knowledge

1 Who am I? I am the head of the Roman Catholic church. ____________

2 A trident is a spear. How many prongs does a trident have? ____________

3 I am an event in Australian history. Gold miners rebelled against the government because of the high price of miners' licences. The event took place in Ballarat, Victoria.

E _ _ _ _ _ S _ _ _ _ _ _ _ _ _

Classroom Unit 25

Plurals: adding s

Your List

pest	pack	frog	train	queen	club	monk	hook
race	scout	goal	bone	apple	trick	plate	bead

____

____

____

RULE: Add *s* to most **nouns** (naming words) to make them **plural** (more than one). For example: one pest—many pests.

1 Re-write the **list** words, on the lines in the box above, as **plurals**.

2 Write the **plurals** of the following words in dictionary order: ***frog***, ***club***, ***race***, ***apple*** and ***bead***. ____

3 Which **list plurals** mean...?

members of a religious group ______________ hiking bags ______________

fruits ______________ we make up the skeleton ______________

4 Which **list plurals** do you:

try to score in a game of netball? ______________

find croaking in a swamp? ______________

compete in at the school sports? ______________

Word Building

Make **compound words** by adding together the words in Group A and the words in Group B.

Group A		Group B		Compound Words
hot	back	clubs	hooks	______________
cup	bull	apples	plates	______________
toffee	night	packs	frogs	______________

Challenge

cheques kiosks shadows serenades guests

Home Study Unit 25

1 Write the following **list** words as **plurals**.

trick ____________	queen ____________	train ____________
plate ____________	pest ____________	club ____________
race ____________	bead ____________	hook ____________
scout ____________	bone ____________	goal ____________

Have you seen
the ghost of Tom?
Long white bones
with the flesh all gone.
OOOOOh!
Wouldn't it be chilly
with no skin on?
(Traditional)

2 Write the **list** words which best fit these pictures.

____________ ____________ ____________ ____________

3 Complete this Wordsearch using the **plurals** of these **list** words.

```
A C S C O U T S T O H
A G U F R O G S R C U
S P K I L V K E A H S
S O P G H A N H I E S
L N C L U B S O N I K
A T S P E C E O S J N
O F R E H S B K O L O
G I P A C K S S Y D M
```

apple	hook
bone	monk
club	pack
frog	scout
goal	train

Word Knowledge

Which **list plurals** or **challenge** words best fit the following groups?

Elizabeth, Mary, Queen of Hearts ____________

flies, mosquitoes, snails, feral cats ____________

Granny Smith, Golden Delicious, Jonathan ____________

songs, ballads, lullabies ____________

General Knowledge

1 What do tadpoles turn into? ____________

2 What do we call signed pieces of paper used as money? ____________

3 In Australian Rules football, how many points equal ten goals? ____________

Classroom Unit 26

Plurals: –s –ss –sh –ch –x –z

Your List

bus	rich	torch	itch	witch	ditch
loss	miss	pass	cross	boss	box
ash	rash	rush	wash	crash	buzz

____

____

____

RULE: When **nouns** (naming words) end with ***s***, ***ss***, ***sh***, ***ch***, ***x*** and ***z***, add ***es*** to make the word **plural**. For example: one crash—several crashes.

1 Re-write the **list** words, on the lines in the box above, as **plurals**.

2 Which **list plurals** mean…?

vehicles for transporting people ____________ wealth ____________

swamp or riverbank plants ____________ people in charge ____________

the remains of a fire ____________ bright lights ____________

3 Choose a **list plural** to write in the gaps in these sentences.

The coach told the players that their long streak of _ _ _ _ _ _ was because of so many _ _ _ _ _ _ _ in front of goal.

Aladdin kept his fabulous _ _ _ _ _ _ _ in _ _ _ _ _ _ made of gold.

Word Building

Complete this table.

miss	missed	missing	misses
pass	______	passing	______
buzz	buzzed	______	______
rush	______	______	rushes
itch	______	______	______
box	______	______	______
wash	______	______	______

Look for smaller words.
For example:
witches = it itch itches
washes = was as ash ashes.

Challenge

radishes churches

Home Study Unit 26

> Faster than fairies, faster than witches,
> Bridges and houses, hedges and ditches.
> (R. L. Stevenson)

1 Write the following **list** words as **plurals**.

wash ____________ buzz ____________ miss ____________ torch ____________

witch ____________ box ____________ rash ____________ bus ____________

2 Which **list** words best fit these pictures?

________________ ________________ ________________

3 Write in dictionary order: ***boxes***, ***buses***, ***buzzes*** and ***bosses***.

____________ ____________ ____________ ____________

4 Write an interesting sentence using: ***witches*** and ***itches***.

____

5 Write the **list plurals** to fill the gaps in this sentence.

At the end of the day the drivers parked their _ _ _ _ _ in the yard, collected their lunch _ _ _ _ _ and then showed their special _ _ _ _ _ _ _ to the _ _ _ _ _ _ _.

Word Knowledge

Choose **list** or **challenge plurals** to complete these groups.

jewels, gold, coins ____________ turnips, parsnips, carrots ____________

trams, trains, taxis ____________ wizards, warlocks, sorcerers, hags ____________

drones, hums, moans ____________

General Knowledge

1 What are we? We are found in the vegetable garden. The part of us that you eat grows underground. We are hot to eat. r_ _ _ _ _ _ _ _

2 For which trophy do England and Australia play Test cricket? ____________

Classroom Unit 27 Plurals: y to i and add es

Your List

cry	baby	story	puppy	daddy
fly	lady	party	mummy	fairy

____

____

____

RULE: For **nouns** (naming words) ending in a **consonant** followed by a ***y***, there are two steps to follow. Change the ***y*** to ***i*** and then add ***es***.
For example: one cry—many cries.

1 Re-write the **list** words, on the lines in the box above, as **plurals**.

2 Which **list plurals** are opposites (**antonyms**) for the following…?

laughs ______________ gentlemen ______________ adults ______________

3 Use **list plurals** to help you finish these sentences.

As we walked into the house we could hear ____________ for help coming from the attic.

Do you believe that ______________ live under toadstools?

Of the many funny ____________ that my teacher read to me, my favourite was one about how to stop annoying ____________ bothering you at birthday ______________.

4 Which **list plurals** mean the same (**synonyms**) as these…?

mothers ______________ dogs ______________

fathers ______________ celebrations ______________

Word Building

Complete:

one baby; several ______________ a puppy; a litter of ______________

a fly; a mass of ______________ one cry; many ______________

one party; two ______________ a fairy; a troop of ______________

Challenge

butterflies dairies diaries juries countries

There are fairies at the bottom of our garden!
They often have a dance on summer nights:
The butterflies and bees make a lovely little breeze,
And the rabbits stand about and hold lights.

(Rose Fyleman)

1 Use the **list plurals**, **challenge** words and clues to help you solve this Crossword.

Across

1 books for daily events
4 little children
6 celebrations
7 tales

Down

1 places where milk is stored
2 females
3 fathers
5 shouts

2 Which **list plurals**…?

__ u __ p __ __ s   b __ b __ __ __   __ a i __ i __ __   __ l __ __ __

Word Knowledge

Change the following words to the **plural** form and then write each in a sentence.

butterfly ____________________

diary ____________________

dairy ____________________

jury ____________________

country ____________________

General Knowledge

Do you know the names of the babies of the following creatures?

dogs __________ bears __________ sheep __________

horses __________ rabbits __________ butterflies __________

Classroom Unit 28

Plurals: vowel followed by y

Your List

key	day	joy	bay	toy	clay	monkey
way	ray	tray	play	boy	delay	donkey

____

____

____

RULE: For **nouns** (naming words) ending in ***y*** following a **vowel** (a e i o u), make the word **plural** by adding ***s***. For example: one ray—many rays.

1 Re-write the **list** words, on the lines in the box above, as **plurals**.

2 Which **list** words mean...?

male children ____________ playthings ____________ pleasures ____________

inlets ____________ poor soils ____________ shafts of light ____________

3 Use **list plurals** to fill the gaps in these sentences.

The actors had appeared in many fine ____________.

Bonny and Corin were woken by brilliant ____________ of sunshine streaming into their bedroom.

There are seven ____________ in one week.

Captain Kincaid tried all of the ____________ in the lock of the treasure chest but none would unlock it.

4 Which **list plurals** are we?

We are used to carry dishes, plates and cups. ____________

We are used for undoing locks. ____________

We are horselike animals. ____________

Word Building

Join the words shown to make new words. Your new words will be **compound words**.

birth + days = ____________ sick + bays = ____________

high + ways = ____________ pay + days = ____________

road + ways = ____________ X- + rays = ____________

Challenge

holidays birthdays drays decoys journeys

Donkeys in a herd will groom themselves in the same way as monkeys.

(Fact)

1 Which **list plurals** best fit these pictures?

____________ ____________ ____________

2 Write in one sentence: ***keys*** and ***boys***.

____

3 Write **list plurals** that rhyme with the following words:

bays ________________________________

joys ________________________________

Word Knowledge

Which **list plurals** or **challenge** words best fit into these groups?

theatres, stages, directors _ _ _ _ _ _

Monday, Tuesday, Friday _ _ _ _ _

bolts, chains, padlocks _ _ _ _ _

lures, traps, snares _ _ _ _ _ _ _

General Knowledge

1 What was the name given to the low carts, without sides, which were used for hauling logs, wool bales and other heavy loads through the bush? _ _ _ _ _ _

2 What are we? Proboscis, Howler, Spider, Macaque, Marmoset

_ _ _ _ _ _ _ _

3 What are we? Port Phillip, Westernport, Botany, Batemans, Byron _ _ _ _ _

Classroom Unit 29 Plurals: –s –ss –sh –ch –x –z

Your List

gas	kiss	grass	glass	fox
bush	wish	dish	push	fizz
catch	bench	bunch	punch	

____

____

____

RULE: When **nouns** (naming words) end with *s*, *ss*, *sh*, *ch*, *x* and *z*, make the word plural by adding *es*. For example: one bunch—several bunches.

1 Re-write the **list** words, on the lines in the box above, as **plurals**.

2 Re-write the **list** words in plurals in dictionary order: ***fizz***, ***grass***, ***push*** and ***gas***.

__________ __________ __________ __________

3 Choose a **list plural** to write in the gap in each sentence.

The only thing that Jerry hated about visiting Aunt Mabel was being smothered by __________.

The children were asked to wash all of the __________ before watching television.

Harry had won the cricket trophy for taking the most number of __________ in the season.

Word Building

Complete this table.

kiss	kissed	kissing	kisses
wish	__________	wishing	__________
fizz	fizzed	__________	__________
punch	__________	__________	__________

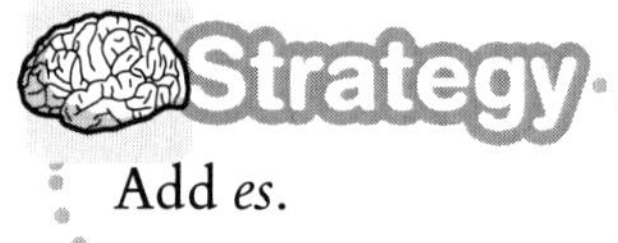

Add *es*.

Challenge

atlases
squashes
cutlasses
screeches
ostriches

If wishes were horses, beggars would ride.
(Proverb)

1 Which **list plurals** fit into these Wordframes?

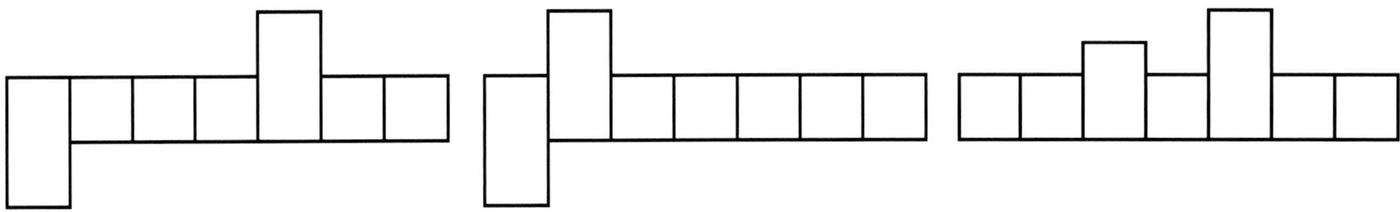

2 Write one sentence using any two **list plurals**.

____

3 Write **list plurals** for each of these pictures.

______________ ______________ ______________

4 Write in dictionary order: ***grasses***, ***punches***, ***foxes*** and ***kisses***.

____

Word Knowledge

1 Which **challenge** words mean…?

books of maps ______________ swords ______________

loud, piercing cries ______________ flightless birds ______________

2 Match a **plural** to the following:

hugs and ______________ dreams and ______________

pulls and ______________ squeals and ______________

General Knowledge

1 In Australia, foxes are feral animals, which are considered pests. Why?

____

2 Can you name any other feral pests?

____

3 What do the following have in common? rye, oats, reeds, buffalo, kikiyu

____

Classroom Unit 30

Plurals: y to i and add es

Your List

spy	army	body	belly	worry	jelly	gully
reply	bully	cherry	berry	city	ruby	lolly

RULE: For **nouns** (naming words) that end in ***y*** following a **consonant**, make the word **plural** by changing the ***y*** to ***i*** and then add ***es***.
For example: one cherry—a basketful of cherries.

1 Re-write the **list** words, on the lines in the box above, as **plurals**.

2 Which **list plurals** mean…?

stomachs ______________ red fruits ______________ troubles ______________

people who mistreat weaker people ______________ groups of soldiers ______________

valuable gemstones ______________ secret watchers ______________

3 Write in dictionary order: ***bodies***, ***cherries***, ***armies***, ***gullies***, ***replies*** and ***jellies***.

____

4 Write **list plurals** in the gaps in these sentences.

The table, at Marnie's birthday party, was covered with cakes, ______________ and wobbly raspberry ____________.

After writing letters to different companies, the children waited for their ______________.

The searchers looked carefully in the ditches and ______________ for the lost bag containing the valuable ______________.

Word Building

Which berries are these?

rasp–	black–	straw-		
cran–	logan–	blue-	+	berries
bramble–	boysen–	goose–		

______________ ______________

______________ ______________

______________ ______________

______________ ______________

____

Challenge

factories families countries
memories strawberries

Bullies are always cowards.
(Proverbs)

1 Write in dictionary order: ***cities***, ***rubies***, ***worries***, ***bellies***, ***lollies*** and ***spies***.

____

2 Which **list plurals** are similar in meaning (**synonyms**) to…?

tummies ____________ answers ____________ sweets ____________

3 There are five **list plurals** hidden in this Wordsearch. Can you find them?

B A B A M I E S G
E A A O G L U L U
L R M S D R U B L
I M R P C I R A L
S I L E H C E A I
E E O I E S B S E
B S L S P I E S S
O C L I E S S R A
D S R E P L I E S
I B E L R E E M S

4 Draw spies hiding behind trees filled with cherries.

Word Knowledge

Write these **challenge** words in sentences to show their meanings.

factories ______________________________

families ______________________________

memories ______________________________

General Knowledge

Which **list** or **challenge** plurals match these groups?

James Bond, undercover, secret agent ____________

blueberry, blackberry, gooseberry ____________

culverts, ditches, creek beds ____________

Melbourne, Sydney, Canberra, Brisbane ____________

emeralds, pearls, diamonds ____________

Plurals

Classroom Review 3

Your List

bean	moss	brush	porch	lily	donkey	rose	try	pony
cloud	class	clash	box	daisy	valley	fairy	study	

1 Re-write the **list** words, on the lines in the box above, as **plurals**.

2 Write these **plurals** in dictionary order: ***clashes***, ***brushes***, ***daisies***, ***valleys*** and ***roses***.

3 Which **list plurals** fit into these Wordframes?

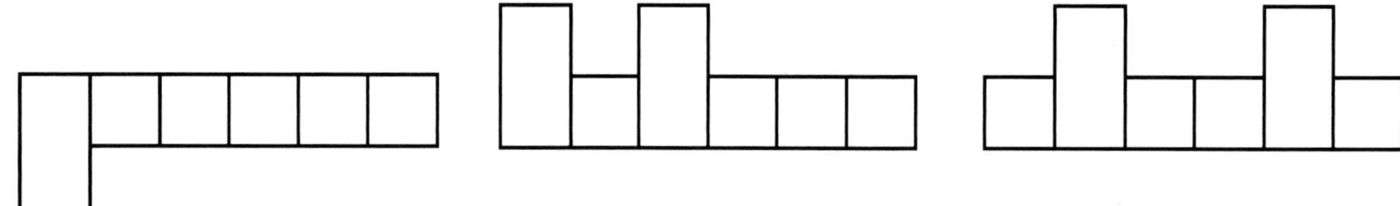

4 Write the **list plurals** that do not end with *es*.

5 Which **list plurals** are flowers?

6 Which **list plurals** begin with *cl*?

7 Which **list plurals**:

can you ride on?

bring rain?

might you sweep with?

Word Building

Which **list plurals** can you add to the following to make new words?

baked _ _ _ _ _ water _ _ _ _ _ _ _

paint _ _ _ _ _ _ _ _ storm _ _ _ _ _ _ _

Challenge

stitches polishes hoaxes beauties centuries

Home Study Review

> Buttercups and daisies,
> Oh, the pretty flowers;
> Coming 'ere the Springtime,
> To tell of sunny hours.
>
> (Mary Howitt)

1 Write **list plurals** for each of these pictures.

_______________ _______________ _______________

2 Write one sentence using any three **list plurals**.

____

3 Write these **list** words as **plurals**.

class _______________ donkey _______________

clash _______________ pony _______________

box _______________ rose _______________

Word Knowledge

Which **list plurals** best fit these groups?

potatoes, peas, carrots _______________

elves, gnomes, goblins _______________

offices, studios, libraries _______________

gullies, gorges, canyons _______________

bumps, impacts, collisions _______________

General Knowledge

1 How many years are there in two centuries? _______________

2 Nimbus, cumulus and stratus cirrus are all _______________.

3 Mules are the offspring from female horses and male _______________.

REMEMBER: YOU CAN ASK SOMEONE TO HELP YOU FIND THE ANSWERS TO THE GENERAL KNOWLEDGE QUESTIONS!

Classroom Unit **31**

Homophones

Your List

meet	meat	one	won	saw	sore	see	sea	
son	sun	deer	dear	to	too	two	for	four
weak	week	tale	tail	rowed	road	rode	sail	sale
maid	made	hear	here					

1 Draw a circle around the correct word.
We did not (hear/here) our teacher ask us to leave our books in a pile (hear/here).
Danny (one/won) (one/won) hundred dollars in the lottery.
As the police (rowed/rode/road) their horses along the rocky (rowed/rode/road), the bushrangers quickly (rowed/rode/road) their boats upstream.

2 Write the **list** word that means:

flesh used for food ____________ come face to face with ____________

the star that gives us heat and light ____________ a male child ____________

not strong ____________ seven days ____________

the end of some animals' backbones ____________ a story ____________

3 Circle the word that fits the picture. saw sore for four see sea

4 Circle the correct word.
one more than one to/too/two
as well as to/too/two
in the direction of to/too/two

Word Building

Match words from the groups to form new **compound words**.

see	sea	+	sighed	side	____________
sail	sale	+	board	bored	____________
rain	rein	+	deer	dear	____________

Strategy

Use memory clues.
For example:
Eat meat.
Hear with your ear.
Four letters in four.

Challenge

stake	steak	steal	steel	tied
tide	hoarse	horse	great	grate
bare	bear	waist	waste	

Home Study Unit 31

There's none so deaf as those who will not hear.
(Proverb)

1 Use the **homophones** shown to complete this Wordsearch.

A	B	C	H	E	R	E	M	O	G	M	S	A
S	G	I	D	O	E	F	E	I	H	E	S	S
A	P	A	N	M	W	E	A	K	E	E	O	A
I	M	U	V	R	A	F	T	B	A	T	U	L
L	W	E	E	K	P	I	C	D	R	I	S	E
D	E	A	R	O	P	F	D	E	E	R	P	Y

weak	week
meet	meat
maid	made
deer	dear
hear	here
sail	sale

2 Which **list** words fit into these Wordframes?

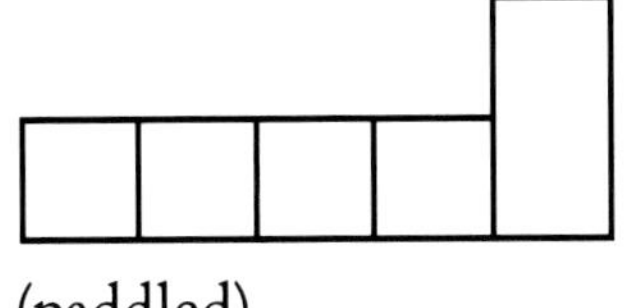
(paddled)

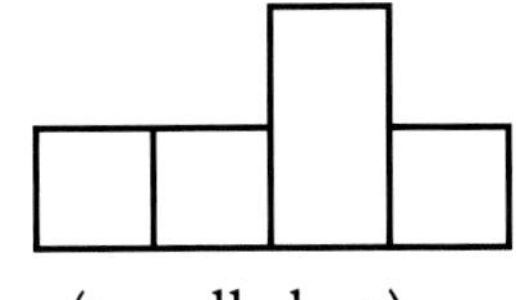
(travelled on)

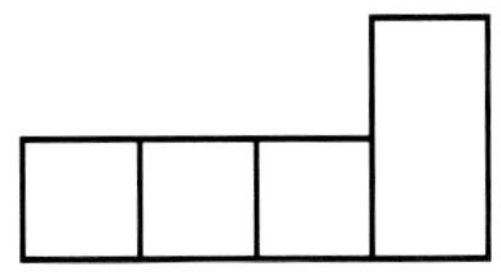
(lane, highway etc.)

3 Which **list** words best fit these pictures?

deer *or* dear

sail *or* sale

son *or* sun

Word Knowledge

Which **challenge** words mean…?

a piece of meat ______________ a wild animal ______________

to take something that does not belong to you ______________

animal used for riding ______________ a metal grid ______________

the area between the chest and hips ______________

General Knowledge

Underline the correct word.

1 Noah built me to escape world-wide floods. (arc/ark)

2 I am a Mediterranean country. (Greece/Grease)

3 I am the rise and fall of the sea. (tide/tied)

Classroom Unit 32

Compound Words

Your List

football	ice-cream	postcard	snowball	outback	cowboy	bedroom	lookout
weekend	sunrise	railway	see-saw	backbone	farmyard	bathroom	bushfire
trapdoor	everyone	blowfly	rainbow	seasick	upset	everything	windmill

1 Which **list** words…?

I appear after rain as an arc of many colours. ____________________

I am another name for the spine. ____________________

Feeling ill because of the movement of water. ____________________

I am an insect. ____________________

2 Write in an interesting sentence the words: ***sunrise*** and ***bedroom***. ________________

____

3 Which **list** words can be made from…?

blwfy ________________ wknd ________________ snwbll ________________

ssck ________________ tbck ________________ cwby ________________

4 Write these compound words in dictionary order: ***see-saw***, ***upset***, ***lookout***, ***postcard*** and ***trapdoor***.

____

Word Building

The word *way* means the course of travel. Add *way* to these words to make new words.

road __ __ __ rail __ __ __ high __ __ __

path __ __ __ free __ __ __ lane __ __ __

alley __ __ __ by __ __ __ water __ __ __

Remember:
A **compound word** is made up of two or more words.

Challenge

jellyfish
toothpaste
earthquake
air conditioner
skateboard

Home Study Unit 32

Everyone speaks well of the bridge that carries him over.
(Proverb)

1 Which two **list** words fit into this Wordframe?

_______________ and _______________

2 Which **list** words do you think of when you read these words?

dessert _______________ morning _______________

hot summer _______________ playground _______________

Saturday and Sunday _______________ winter _______________

holiday news _______________ scenic view _______________

3 Draw an upset blowfly sitting on a rainbow, and a cowboy kicking a snowball shaped like a football.

Word Knowledge

Match these meanings with the **challenge** words:

a room cooler _______________ cleanser for the teeth _______________

flat board with wheels _______________ a sea creature _______________

Choose one of the **challenge** words and write it in an interesting sentence.

____

General Knowledge

1 What am I? I am another name for an echidna.

_ _ _ _ _   _ _ _ _ _ _ _ _ _

2 What am I? I am a musical instrument. I am blown, and at the same time squeezed.

I am common in Scotland. _ _ _ _ _ _ _ _ _ _

3 I am the name given to Australian outlaws who lived in the bush. Ned Kelly was

a well-known one. _ _ _ _ _ _ _ _ _ _ _ _ _ _ _

Classroom Unit **33**

Contractions

Your List

she's	they're	we're	you're	he's	we'll
I'd	I've	don't	we've	I'll	I'm

A **contraction** is made when we join two words together, but we leave out some of the letters. The missing letters are replaced with an **apostrophe** (').
For example: we'll = we will.

1 Match the **list** words with these words :

I am ___________ we have ___________ do not ___________

she is ___________ they are ___________ I have ___________

he is ___________ I had ___________ we will ___________

you are ___________ we are ___________ I will ___________

2 Write an interesting sentence using the words: ***I'm*** and ***they're***.

____

3 Write the **list** words which best fit the gaps in these sentences.

'If we ___________ hurry ___________ be late again,' cried Mum.

Marie is coming with us on the picnic and ___________ bringing a drink too.

'Do you know what ___________ going to get for your birthday, Bobby?' asked Tim.

'___________ the fastest runner in the land,' boasted the Prince. 'No one can run faster than I can.'

Word Building

Complete these **list** words.

__ h e' __ d __ __'t

w __ 'v __ __ e' r __ I' __ e

w __ 'l __ __ h e __ ' __ e

The **apostrophe** takes the place of one or more missing letters.

Challenge

could've
wasn't
wouldn't

> Two wrongs don't make a right.
> (Proverb)

1 Which **list** words mean…?

we have ____________ we will ____________ do not ____________

you are ____________ she is ____________ I had ____________

2 Write an interesting sentence using: ***he's*** and ***I'm***.

____

3 Write out these **list** words in full:

I've _ _ _ _ _ they're _ _ _ _ _ _ _ _

we're _ _ _ _ _ _ he's _ _ _ _ _ I'm _ _ _

I'll _ _ _ _ _

4 Use a **list** word to fill in the gaps in these sentences:

Monkeys ____________ like water.

____________ be leaving as soon as our bus comes.

When ____________ feeling unwell, sleep is the best thing for you.

If ____________ the King, then she must be the Queen.

5 Which **challenge** words match…?

would not ____________ could have ____________ was not ____________

Word Knowledge

Homophones are words which sound the same but are spelt differently and have different meanings.
Write **list** words which are **homophones** for:

weave ____________ wheel ____________ their ____________

General Knowledge

1 Who am I?
I'm a fairytale character. I broke into a family's cottage, ate some of their food, broke a chair and slept in one of their beds. ____________________________

2 Who are we?
We're hardworking fairytale people who looked after a beautiful princess whose stepmother thought she was too beautiful. ____________________________

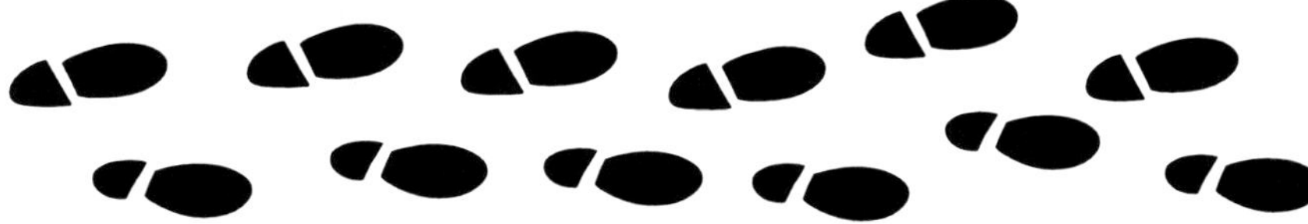

Classroom Unit 34 Homographs

Your List

fair	kind	lie	pick	ring	pen
free	bark	lap	dear	row	trip
duck	fly	bowl	light	like	well

1 Which **list** words mean…?

expensive *or* much loved _ _ _ _

light-coloured *or* honest _ _ _ _

a two-winged insect *or* move through the air _ _ _

dog's noise *or* outer skin of a tree _ _ _ _

a circle *or* a piece of jewellery _ _ _ _

not heavy *or* bright and clear _ _ _ _ _

a line of something *or* paddle _ _ _

a place to keep sheep *or* a writing instrument _ _ _

2 Write **list** words for each of these pictures.

3 Match the following words with **list** words which are **synonyms**. (A **synonym** is a word with a similar meaning to another word.)

type ____________ untruth ____________ journey ____________

generous ____________ tool ____________ select ____________

4 Write an interesting sentence showing both the meanings of ***well***.

____

Word Building

Add the endings shown to the **list** words.

lap + ing (*careful*) _ _ _ _ _ _ _

free + dom _ _ _ _ _ _ _

kind + ness _ _ _ _ _ _ _ _

bowl + er _ _ _ _ _ _

trip + ing (*careful*) _ _ _ _ _ _ _ _

pick + ing _ _ _ _ _ _ _

pen + ed (*careful*) _ _ _ _ _ _

light + en _ _ _ _ _ _ _

Challenge

cricket fleet crane board bound

Home Study Unit 34

1 Use **list** words and the clues to help you solve this Crossword.

Across

2 honest, or light-coloured
3 send a ball along the ground, or a dish
5 expensive, or loved one
6 type, or generous
7 top of legs when sitting, or around a course once, or lick liquid with a tongue
9 similar to, or to find pleasant
10 not heavy, or brightness

Down

1 costing nothing, or not caught
2 insect, or move through the air
3 tree's skin, or dog's noise
4 fall over something, or journey
7 an untruth, or rest
8 circle, or jewellery

2 Draw a duck ducking, a bowling bowl or a cricket playing cricket.

Word Knowledge

Which **list** words match these groups?

bulb, candle, torch, flame ____________

catch, throw, roll ____________

soar, wing, glide ____________

feather, balloon, leaf ____________

dragon–, blow–, house–, sand–, horse– ____________

dish, plate, tray ____________

General Knowledge

What am I?

1 I can be a wading bird or a machine for lifting heavy objects. _ _ _ _ _

2 I can be a game or an insect that makes a chirping sound. _ _ _ _ _ _ _

3 I can mean tied up or a leap or jump. _ _ _ _ _

4 I can mean very quick or I can be a group of ships. _ _ _ _ _

Compound Words

Your List

daydream	backfire	spaceship	playground	backyard	fairytale	whenever
bushwalk	outlaw	thankyou	toadstool	peacock	pipeline	fortnight
airport	homesick	outside	sunshine	tiptoe	woodwork	footstep

1 Write in dictionary order: ***backfire***, ***outlaw***, ***fortnight***, ***backyard*** and ***daydream***.

____

2 Which **list** words fit into these Wordframes?

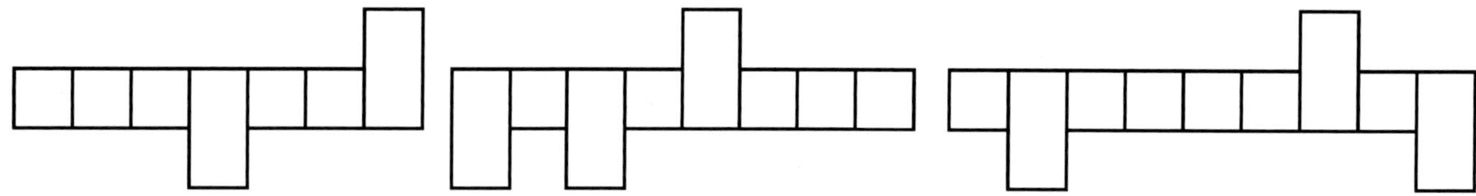

3 Which **list** words mean…?

a story __ __ __ __ __ __ __ __ __ a bird with a beautiful tail __ __ __ __ __ __ __

a pace __ __ __ __ __ __ __ __ creeping walk __ __ __ __ __ __

missing home __ __ __ __ __ __ __ __ a fungus __ __ __ __ __ __ __ __ __

4 Which **list** word is an **antonym** for inside? __ __ __ __ __ __ __

5 Which **list** word is a **synonym** for carpentry? __ __ __ __ __ __ __ __

6 True or False?

someone who is homesick is sick of homes ________

a pipeline is a line of pipes ________

a bushwalk is a walk in the bush ________

a fortnight is night time in a fort ________

Word Building

Backfire and *backyard* are just two **compound words** that use ***back*** as the **base word**. How many others can you find? (Use a dictionary or wordlist to help you.)

____

Challenge

butterfly grasshopper keyboard lighthouse silverfish

Home Study Unit 35

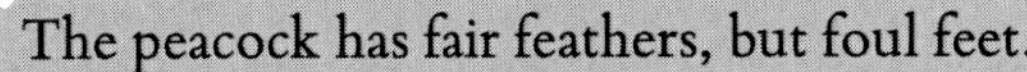

The peacock has fair feathers, but foul feet.
(Proverb)

1 Which **list** words do these words best match up with?

fourteen days ______________

see-saw, slide, swing ______________

shuttle, rocket, capsule ______________

saw, hammer, nails ______________

Snow White, Cinderella, Rumpelstiltskin ______________

jumbo, control tower, runway ______________

2 Write a **list** word in the gap in each sentence.

The elf crept across the forest floor on _ _ _ _ _ _ _ _ _.

The farmers were pleased to see some _ _ _ _ _ _ _ _ _ _ _ _ _ _ _ after all the rain.

Before going on an overnight _ _ _ _ _ _ _ _ _ _ _ _ _ _ _ you should let someone know where you will be walking.

Billy had only been away for two hours when he started to feel _ _ _ _ _ _ _ _ _ _ _ _ _.

3 Draw a spaceship on a toadstool.

Word Knowledge

What am I? Choose answers from the **challenge** words.

I am used to signal ships at sea. ______________

I grow from a caterpillar into a beautiful insect. ______________

The two things that I am best at are jumping and singing. ______________

I am used to type information into a computer. ______________

I am an insect that eats paper. ______________

General Knowledge

1 What do the following people have in common?

Ned Kelly   Dan Morgan   the Wild Colonial Boy   Martin Cash

____

2 What name is given to the two wooden sticks used in Asian countries for eating?

____

Classroom Unit 36 Contractions (Review)

Your List

we're	I'll	we've	you're	I've	she's
I'm	he's	we'll	I'd	don't	they're

A **contraction** is made when we join two words together, but we leave out some of the letters. The missing letters are replaced with an **apostrophe** (').
For example: we're = we are.

1 Write these **list** words in dictionary order: ***I'll***, ***he's***, ***I'd***, ***don't*** and ***we'll***.

____

2 Match the **list contractions** with the full words.

we're	________	they are	________
I'm	________	he is	________
they're	________	we are	________
you're	________	I had	________
we've	________	we have	________
he's	________	you are	________
I'd	________	I am	________

3 Write one sentence for each of these words.

we'll ______________________________

she's ______________________________

don't ______________________________

4 Which **list** words fit these Wordframes?

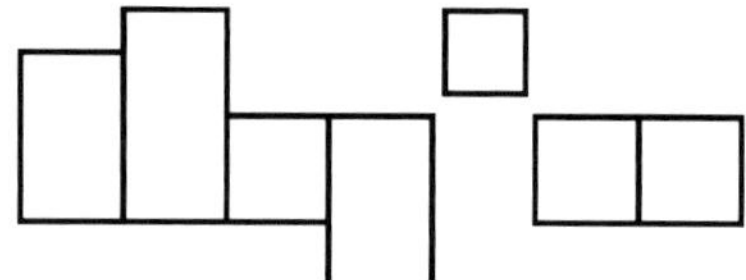

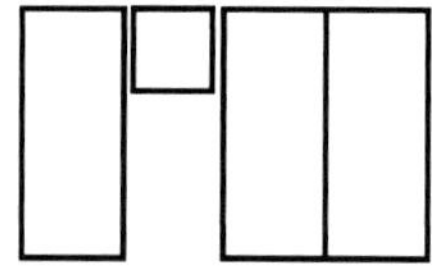

Word Building

Write in full.

I've ________	you're ________
don't ________	I'm ________
they're ________	she's ________

Challenge
doesn't didn't

Home Study Unit 36

Don't count your chickens before they're hatched.
(Proverb)

1 Use the clues to help you complete this Crossword.

Across	**Down**
1 they're	2 he's
5 she's	3 you're
7 we're	4 we've
8 I'll	6 we'll

2 Which **list** words…?

I have ____________ I am ____________

I had ____________ do not ____________

3 Write the letter for each school rule on the correct lines.

a line up quickly when the bell rings

b treat others with kindness

c drop your lunch papers on the oval

d run in the corridors

e ride bikes in the Prep playground

f be helpful to the infant children

Do ________________________ **Don't** ________________________

Word Knowledge

Write all the **list** and **challenge** words in groups according to their **base words**.

Base Words	**Contractions**			
we	________	________	________	
I	________	________	________	________
do	________	________	________	
you	________			
he	________			
she	________			
they	________			

General Knowledge

What am I?

1 I'm the fastest land animal. ____________________

2 I'm the largest land creature. ____________________

3 I'm the largest sea creature. ____________________

4 I'm the smallest bird. ____________________

Compound Words/Homonyms/Contractions

Classroom Review 4

Your List

hear	here	rainbow	sail	sale	row	football	pen
they're	there	their	weave	we've	well	there's	bedroom
week	weak	bushfire	weekend	don't	whatever	whenever	

1 Which **list** words are **homophones** for the following words?

hear ____________ sale ____________ they're ____________

weak ____________ weave ____________

2 Which **list homographs** mean…?

to paddle *or* a line of something ____________

an animal's home *or* a writing instrument ____________

a drilled hole where water, oil or gas can be found *or* to be in a good way ____________

3 Complete these **compound words**.

bush ____________ foot ____________ week ____________

____________ room ____________ board ____________ bow

4 Write in full.

they're ______________ don't ______________ we've ______________

5 Write each of these words in a sentence to show you know their meanings.

their (belonging to them) ______________________________

there (in that place) ______________________________

they're (they are) ______________________________

Word Building

Add a **list** word to the following to make a new word.

_ _ _ _ end _ _ _ _ –known over _ _ _ _

_ _ _ _ ling _ _ _ _ _ fore

_ _ _ _ board un _ _ _ _

Challenge

they've	piece	peace	through	threw
cupboard	you've	chest	file	afternoon

All's well that ends well.
(Proverb)

1 Use **list** words to label the following pictures.

2 Circle the correct word in these sentences.
Can you (hear/here) the approaching thunderstorm? It will soon be (here/hear).
After the (sale/sail), at which I bought a new yacht, I set off to (sale/sail) around the world.
(They're/their/there) is a story about a Teddy Bears' picnic in which the bears ate all of (they're/their/there) chocolate too quickly. Now (they're/there/their) feeling very ill.
'Today (we've/weave) learnt how to (we've/weave) on a loom,' announced Mr Bryant.

3 Choose three **challenge** words and write each one in a sentence.

Word Knowledge

1 Write the words ***they've*** and ***you've*** in full.

2 Which **challenge** words are **compound words**?

3 Draw a pirate's treasure chest.

4 Draw a pirate with a pirate flag tattooed on his chest.

General Knowledge

1 Which two days make the weekend? ________ and ________

2 What three-lettered word can be the name of a pig's pen? ________

3 Can you list the seven colours of the rainbow? ________

Spelling Reference List

A
abstain
afternoon
again
against
ail
ailment
air conditioner
airport
ale
alight
all right
almost
also
among
antelope
appear
apples
armies
arose
ashes
ashore
astonish
atlases
attack
avail
available
awful
awkward

B
babies
back
backbone
backfire
backyard
bail
bake
bamboo
band
bang
bank
bare
bark
bath
bathroom
bawl
bays
beach
beacon
bead
beads
beak
beam
bean
beans
bear
beard
beast
beauties
became
bedroom
bee
beef
been
bellies
benches
bend
berries
between
bight
billabong
birthdays
black
blank
blast
blight
blind
bloat
block
blot
blow
blowfly
blur
blush
board
boat
bodies
bone
bones
book
boom
boomerang
boot
bore
bosses
bound
bow
bowl
boxes
boys
brain
branch
brave
brawl
brick
bright
brim
bring
brink
brook
brother
brow
brown
brush
brushes
bullies
bunches
burst
buses
bush
bushes
bushfire
bushwalk
butterflies
butterfly
buzzes

C
cage
cake
came
campaign
candlestick
canine
canteen
captain
carnivore
cash
catches
cave
cent
centuries
chain
chainsaw
chalk
challenge
champion
chance
chapel
char
charcoal
chat
cheat
cheques
cherries
cherry
chess
chest
chew
chicken
chief
child
chill
chimney
chin
chip
chisel
chocolate
chop
chore
chose
church
churches
cities
clap
clash
clashes
classes
claw
clay
clays
clean
clear
clergy
clever
click
clock
close
cloth
clouds
clown
club
clubs
clumsy
coal
coat
coax
cockatoo
complain
compose
cone
console
contain
contest
cook
coop
core
cost
could've
countries
cow
cowboy
cowl

crab
crack
crane
crash
crashes
crawl
crayon
creak
creature
creek
crew
cricket
cries
crimson
croak
crook
crosses
crowd
crown
crush
cupboard
cutlasses
cyclone

D

daddies
daily
dainty
dairies
daisies
date
dawdle
dawn
daydream
days
dear
deck
decline
decoys
deed
deep
deer
defeat
define
delays
delight
demean
dentist
depend
depth
descend
detail
detain
diagnose
diaries
didn't
dine
dish
dishes
dispose
ditches
divine
dock
doesn't
don't
donkey
doom
dowdy
down
drain
drama
draw
drawers
drawl
drays
dream
dreary
drop
drown
drum
duck
dumbstruck
dust

E

each
ear
earthquake
earwig
east
Easter
eat
educate
eighth
elephant
eleventh
embrace
enclose
encore
endear
engage
enlist
enrage
entertain
everyone
everything
exceed
excellent
exhale
exist
expand
explain
explore
expose
eyesight

F

face
factories
fade
fail
failure
faint
fair
fairies
fairytale
fake
families
fang
farmyard
fast
fawn
fear
feast
fee
feed
feet
feline
female
fifteen
fifth
fight
file
filth
find
fine
finish
first
fish
fist
fizzes
flag
flame
flamingo
flash
flat
flaw
flea
flee
fleet
flesh
flies
flight
flimsy
fling
float
florist
fly
foal
foam
folklore
food
fool
foot
football
footstep
for
fore
forest
fortnight
four
fourth
fowl
foxes
frail
free
fresh
Friday
friend
fright
frog
frogs
front
frost
frown

G

gain
gale
game
gases
gate
gave
gawk
gear
giant
girth
glacier
glad
glasses
gleam
glee
gloom
glory
glove
glow
glucose
glum
gnash
gnaw
goad
goal
goals
goat
good
goodbye
gore
gown
grab
grade

grain
graph
grasses
grasshopper
grate
great
green
grey
grin
grind
grip
gripe
groan
grocer
growl
growth
grunt
guest
guests
gullies

H
hacksaw
hail
hang
harsh
harvest
hate
hawk
he's
hear
hearth
heed
herbivore
here
high
highlight
hoarse
hoax
hoaxes
hole
holidays
homesick
honest
hood
hoodwink
hoof
hook
hooks
hoop
hoot
hope
horse
hose
howl

I
I'd
I'll
I'm
I've
ice-cream
incline
indeed
inhale
insight
interest
intestine
invade
investigate
itches
its

J
jail
jaw
jellies
jellyfish
journeys
jowl
joys
juries

K
kangaroo
keen
keep
keyboard
keys
kick
kind
king
kiosks
kisses
knight
knock
kookaburra

L
lace
ladies
land
lap
last
late
law
lawn
lawyer
length
lie
light
lighthouse
lightning
like
likelihood
lilies
limelight
limerick
line
list
livestock
load
loaf
loam
loathe
locate
lock
lollies
lone
long
look
lookout
loop
loot
losses
lost
luck

M
made
maid
mail
main
make
male
mate
mean
meat
meek
meet
memories
mend
midnight
might
mind
mine
mirth
misses
mist
mistake
moan
mole
monkey
monks
mood
moon
more
mosses
most
mummy
must
myth

N
nail
name
near
nearly
neck
need
nest
nigh
night
nightingale
nine
ninth
nook
noon
north
nose
nuclear

O
oak
oat
obtain
omnivore
one
or
ore
ostriches
outback
outlaw
outside

P
packs
page
pail
pain
paint
pale
parade
parties
passes
past
path
paw
pea
peace
peacock
peck
peep
pen
pests
pick
piece
pine
pink
pipe

pipeline
pith
place
plain
plan
planet
plank
plant
platypus
play
playground
plays
plea
plenty
plight
plot
pluck
plug
pole
polishes
ponies
pool
porches
pore
pose
post
postcard
postpone
pray
preach
prepare
prey
print
prison
problem
product
prolong
prong
proper
propose
prowl
punches
punish
puppy
push
pushes

Q

quail
quaint
queens
quick

R

race
races
rack
radishes
rage
rail
railway
rain
rainbow
ransack
rashes
raw
rays
reach
read
ream
rear
reed
reek
refund
renown
repeat
replies
reprimand
restore
restrain
retail
retain
retreat
rich
riches
right
ring
ripe
rissole
road
roam
rock
rode
roof
rook
room
root
rope
roses
row (cow)
row (go)
rowed
rubbish
rubies
rush
rushes
rust

S

sack
sail
sailor
saint
sale
same
sand
save
saw
scale
scent
school
score
scouts
scowl
scrawl
scream
screeches
sea
sear
seasick
seat
second
see
seed
seek
seem
seen
see-saw
selfish
send
sent
serenades
seventh
shade
shadow
shadows
shallow
shampoo
shawl
she's
shear
shell
shine
ship
shipwreck
shock
shore
shovel
show
shrine
shut
sick
sigh
sight
silverfish
sing
sixth
skateboard
skeleton
ski
skill
skin
skull
sky
slack
slap
sleuth
slight
slim
slip
slope
slot
slouch
slow
smack
small
smear
smell
smog
smuggler
snack
snag
snail
snake
snap
snip
snipe
snore
snow
snowball
snug
soak
soap
son
soon
sore
sow
space
spaceship
spaghetti
speak
spear
spell
spend
spider
spies
spin
spine
spirit
spool
spore
spot
sprawl
squashes
squeak
stage
stain
stake
stale
stand
stay

steak
steal
steam
steel
step
stew
stick
still
stir
stitches
stock
stole
stomach
stone
stood
stop
store
storey
stories
story
strain
straw
strawberries
strawberry
stream
stripe
stuck
studies
studio
succeed
suggest
sun
sunrise
sunshine
suppose
surname
swan
sway
swerve
swim
swine
swing
swipe

T

tail
tailor
take
tale
tame
tank
tattoo
tawny
tea
teach
team
tear
teeth
tent
tenth
test
than
thank
thankyou
that
thaw
the
their
them
themselves
then
there
there's
therefore
these
they
they're
they've
thigh
think
this
those
though
three
threw
throne
through
thumbnail
tide
tied
tight
tiptoe
to
toad
toadstool
tone
too
took
tool
tooth
toothpaste
torches
tore
towel
town
toys
track
trail
train
trains
tram
trap
trapdoor
travel
trawl
trays
tree
trial
tricks
tries
trip
tripe
trombone
trot
truck
trunk
trust
turbine
tweezers
twelfth
twilight
twine
two

U

ungainly
until
upset

V

vain
valleys
vanish
varnish
vine
viper
vow

W

wade
wage
wail
waist
want
wash
washes
wasn't
waste
wave
ways
we'll
we're
we've
weak
wealth
weave
weed
weekend
weep
well
went
west
whale
whatever
whenever
whether
while
whine
whole
whose
windmill
wine
wing
wipe
wish
wishes
witches
withdraw
won
wood
woodwork
wool
woollen
wore
worries
worst
worth
wouldn't
wrap
wrath
wren
written
wrong

X

Y

yawn
year
yet
you're
you've
your

Z

zone

My Personal Word List

Here are some **link words** for you to learn:
until also or whose whether your its yet

Student Profile

At this level the student's knowledge of:

...is	Not Apparent	Emerging	Consolidating	Established
'magic **e**' words				
double **e** words (**ee**)				
double **o** words (**hoop**)				
double **o** words (**book**)				
oa words				
ai words				
ea words				
ow words (**cow**)				
ear words (**rear**)				
aw words (**jaw**)				
igh words				
ight words				
Initial blends: **ch**				
Initial blends: **th**				
Initial blends: **bl pl sl cl gl fl**				
Initial blends: **sm sn sw sk st sp sh**				
Initial blends: **cr gr tr br dr pr fr wr**				
Final blends: **ng nd nt nk**				
Final blends: **st sh**				
Final blends: **ck**				
Final blends: **th**				
Plurals: add **s**				
Plurals: words ending with **s ss ch sh x z**				
Plurals: words ending with **y** following a consonant				
Plurals: words ending with **y** following a vowel				
Homophones				
Homographs				
Compound words				
Contractions				

Comments

Spelling Guide

The English language has grown from many languages so it is difficult to have a set of hard and fast rules for learning to spell.

Rather than being spelling rules, the following is a guide for spelling. Many so-called rules of spelling have exceptions, so it is best to learn the guide and remember the exceptions.

1 To add ***ing*** to words ending with ***e***, drop the ***e*** then add ***ing***.
For example: skate—skating, dodge—dodging, stare—staring, write—writing.

Exceptions:
If there is a vowel before the last ***e***. For example: seeing, canoeing.

2 To add ***ing***, ***ed*** or ***er*** to words ending with a consonant, double the consonant.
For example: stir—stirring; span—spanning; plot—plotting; stop—stopped, stopping; travel—traveller, travelling, travelled; run—runner, running.

Exceptions:

- **a** Words ending with a vowel then ***w***. For example: rowed, screwed, chewing, flowing, growing.
- **b** Words ending with a vowel then ***x***. For example: boxer, boxed, boxing, taxed, fixing.
- **c** Words ending with a vowel then ***y***. For example: saying, annoyed, prayer.
- **d** When there are TWO vowels before the last consonant do not double the last letter. For example: repairing, screening, sleeping, squealed, threaded, treated.

3 Put ***i*** before ***e*** when the sound is ***e*** and they do not follow ***c***.
For example: piece, field, believe, achieve.

Exceptions:
seize

Put ***e*** before ***i*** after ***c***.
For example: receive, ceiling, deceive.

Exceptions:
eight, either, neither, height, weight, freight, weird, rein, their

4 *Plurals*

- **a** Words ending in ***s ss sh ch x z***, add ***es***.
- **b** Words ending in ***y*** following a consonant, change the ***y*** to ***i*** then add ***es***
- **c** Words ending in ***y*** following a vowel, add ***s***.
- **d** Words ending in ***f*** or ***fe*** change ***f*** or ***fe*** to ***v*** then add ***es***.

Exceptions:
chiefs, dwarfs, roofs, gulfs, staffs

- **e** Some words have a change of basic spelling.
- **f** Words ending in ***o*** add ***es***. For example: heroes, potatoes, tomatoes.

Exceptions:
Words from languages other than English. For example: pianos, kimonos.

Glossary

acrostic	a sentence or poem, in which the first letters of the words, or line, spell a word
adjective	a word that describes another (for example: tiny, dark, magnificent)
antonym	a word having the opposite meaning to another
apostrophe	(i) a sign showing a letter (or letters) have been left out (’)
	(ii) a sign showing that something is owned (for example: Terry’s book)
base word	the word from which others may come (for example: circle—circular)
challenge	a group of words that belong to the same family as the list words, but may be more challenging to master
compound word	a word made up of two words (for example: foot + ball = football)
consonant	letters of the alphabet that are not vowels
contraction	shortened form of words in which an apostrophe represents missing letters
homograph	a word that is spelt the same as another word but has a different meaning (for example: bear—carry, bear—animal)
homonym	a word that has the same sound or spelling as another word but a different meaning (for example: right, write)
homophone	two words that sound the same (for example: right, write)
link words	words that help build a sentence and make it more interesting
list words	a group of words with a similarity in spelling
nouns	words that name something (for example: chair, book, country, house)
palindrome	a palindromic word is one that is spelt the same backwards and forwards (for example: noon, madam)
plural	a word that means more than one (for example: bunches, boys, foxes)
prefix	a word part which, when placed in front of a word, changes its meaning (for example: interest + dis = disinterest)
suffix	a word part which, when added to the end of a word, changes its meaning (for example: ness + sad = sadness)
syllable	part of a word that contains a vowel sound or a consonant acting as a vowel (for example: along = a / long)
synonym	a word having a similar meaning to another
verb	a word that tells you about an action (for example: walk, hear)
vowel	the letters *a e i o u*

Spelling Matters—Book 3 (3rd Edition) Answers

Unit	Page	Answers
1	6	**1** face, race, lace, space, place mate, late, date, gate, hate **2** bake, cage, date, fade, gave **3** face, space, mate, wade **4** page, stage, wave **WB 1** racing, waving, making, taking, saving, shading **2** spaceship, checkmate, gateway (raceway), shockwave
1	7	**1** shade, snake, space, stage **2** Teacher**3** bake, brave, hate, late **4** Teacher **WK 1** cave, face, rage, hate, flame, name **2** Teacher **GK 1** snake **2** Teacher **3** rake, stake, spade
2	8	**1** tale, male **2** Teacher **3** stale, pale, female **4** Teacher **5** Teacher **WB** wholesale, stalemate, whalebone, telltale, fullscale
2	9	**1** ale, female, gale, sale **2** Teacher **3** gale, tale, nightingale, exhale **4** Teacher **WK 1** bail, bail, bale **GK 1** gale **2** Airedale
3	10	**1** line, nine, pine, vine **2** ripe, dine, wipe, pipe, spine, swipe **3** Teacher **4** whine, wine **5** Teacher **WB** pineapple, ninety, spinal
3	11	**1** pipe, ripe, wine, wipe **2** swine, turbine, viper, intestine **3** *Across:* 1 twine 4 pine 5 vine *Down:* 2 wipe 3 nine **GK 1** serpentine like a serpent, feline like a cat, elephantine like an elephant, leonine like a lion, equine like a horse, porcine like a pig, tigrine like a tiger **2** three stripes on the sleeve
4	12	**1** chore, restore, fore, ore, sore, ashore, shore, core **2** bore, sore, store, tore, wore **3** Teacher **WB** forearm, foretell, forefinger, foreseen, forehead, foreground
4	13	**1** Teacher **2** Teacher **3** boring, snoring, exploring **WK** Teacher **GK 1** spore **2** carnivore **3** herbivore **4** pore **5** omnivore
5	14	**1** close, stone, slope, pole, whole, hole **2** hose, nose, bone, throne, mole, rose **3** Teacher **4** hope, rope, slope **5** nose, throne, rose, lone **WB** closure, lonely, hopeful, polar, composure, exposure
5	15	**1** close, close rose, rose **2** bone, lone, stone, throne **3** lone, loan whole, hole **4** close, whole, hope **WK** propose, proposal, console, consolation, dispose, disposal **GK 1** composers **2** pole vault **3** glucose
6	16	**1** beef, meek, peep, seek, weed **2** bean/been, meat/meet, weak/week, read/reed **3** Teacher **4** beef, flee, keen, see-saw, bee, canteen, between **5** peep, deed **WB** glee, deep, free, weep, exceed, succeed
6	17	**1** Teacher **2** reed/a swamp grass, read/to look at words and understand them, been/to have existed or to have gone, bean/vegetable, feet/the parts of the body at the end of the legs, feat/a deed of great skill or courage, meet/to come face to face with, meat/animal flesh **3** Teacher **WK** feet **GK 1** fifteen **2** Wednesday

Spelling Matters—Book 3 (3rd Edition) Answers

Unit	Page	Answers
7	18	**1** boot, loot, hoot, root **2** Teacher **3** hoof, cockatoo, kangaroo **4** loot, mood, doom **5** noon **6** two, to to, too **WB** roofs, hooves
7	19	**1** hoof, hoop, loot, mood, moon **2** tool, boom room, noon **3** loot, noon, boot **4** Teacher **WK** waxes, wanes **GK 1** boomerang **2** shampoo **3** bamboo
8	20	**1** Teacher **2** took, nook, rook, hook, brook, cook, book, crook, look wood, hood, good, stood foot wool **3** kookaburra, cook, crook, hood, goodbye **WB 1** took, stood, foot **2** wooden, hooded, crooked
8	21	**1** *Across:* 1 hood 4 kookaburra 7 stood 8 nook *Down:* 1 hook 2 foot 3 brook 5 book 6 cook **2** Teacher **3** football, woodwork, understood **WK** brook, goodbye, look, hoodwink **GK 1** wool **2** Captain Hook **3** wood
9	22	**1** coal, coat, load, loaf **2** toad, oak, roam, foal, soap, boat **3** boat, toad, loaf, goal **4** oat, boat, coat, goat **5** croak, moan, groan **WB** rowboat, toadstool, charcoal, oatmeal, roadway, coathanger, goalshooter
9	23	**1** toad, soak, loaf, boat, road **2** Teacher **WK** goad, hoax, bloat, loam, loathe **GK 1** kid **2** tadpole
10	24	**1** detail, snail, trail **2** pail, wail, jail, ail, hail, mail **3** Teacher **WB 1** failing, failed, mailing, mailed, sailing, sailed **2** failure, available
10	25	**1** Teacher **2** hail, jail, mail, nail, pail **3** Teacher **WK 1** thumbnail, railway, toenail, hailstorm **2** a bird **GK 1** tailor, sailor **2** braille
11	26	**1** against, brain, drain, grain, stain **2** brain, strain, grain, drain, train (rain) **3** plain, main, complain, pain **4** Teacher **5** Teacher **WB** drainage, painful, maintain, entertainment
11	27	**1** captain, chain, complain, contain **2** captain, chain, brain, pain, drain **3** contain, captain **WB** restrain, campaign, detain, dainty, abstain, quaint **GK 1** Spain **2** brain **3** Daintree
12	28	**1** defeat/to beat in a contest, cheat/someone who is dishonest, steam/water that is gas, beach/where the sea meets the shore, flea/an insect, feast/a large meal **2** creek, creak, weak, beach **3** neat, speak, mean, east, weak, teach **WB** teamwork, seaside, meanwhile, beachball, beanbag,teatime (teabag), daydream (daytime), meateater
Unit	**Page**	**Answers**

Spelling Matters—Book 3 (3rd Edition) Answers

Unit	Page	Answers
12	29	**1** *Across:* 1 clean 3 reach 4 pea 5 teach 8 team 9 sea 10 weak *Down:* 1 cheat 2 eat 3 repeat 6 creak 7 east **2** weak, read, each **3** Teacher **WK 1** Teacher (seaside, seashore, seasick, sealife, overseas etc.) **2** Easter, creature, ream, beacon, retreat, plea **GK 1** 5 (on court), 11, 13, 18 (on field), 7 (on court), 15 (unless Sevens is being played) **2** lion
13	30	**1** fowl, growl, howl, prowl, scowl **2** bow, row, sow, fowl **3** vow, prowl, clown, dowdy, jowl, renown **4** scowl, crown, frown, brow, jowl **5** Teacher **WB** townhouse, downpour, however, anyhow, township, downfall
13	31	**1** Teacher **2** a hood **WK** howling, clowning, prowling, rowing, growling, vowing,scowling, crowning, bowing, frowning, crowding, drowning **GK 1** The Tower of London **2** boar **3** Harold Holt
14	32	**1** hear, here, deer, sheer, shear, dear **2** dear, dear rear, rear gear, gear **3** fearful, yearly, fearless, nearly, fearsome, clearance, dearest, tearful
14	33	**1** beard, spear, ear, sear, dreary, year **2** Teacher **3** ear, beard, spear **4** dreary, smear, appear **5** appear, near, dear **WK** shear, clear, appear, hear **GK 1** 2012, 2016, 2020, 2024 **2** Edward Lear **3** spiders
15	34	**1** awful, brawl, crawl, shawl, straw, trawl **2** Teacher **3** raw, withdraw, thaw, dawn **4** law, yawn, straw, sprawl, drawers **5** yawn, brawl **WB** jaw, draw/withdraw, straw/strawberry, lawn, crawl, law
15	35	**1** gawk, law, awful **2** Teacher **3** Teacher **WK** Because the fishers trawl a net to catch the fish **GK 1** fawn **2** Henry Lawson **3** Douglas Mawson
16	36	**1** Teacher **2** fight, high, light, nigh, sigh, thigh **3** brightness, not heavy **WB 1** fighting, sighting, delighting, lighting **2** brightening, frightening, tightening, lightening, sighting, frightening
16	37	**1** knight, lightning, light, fright **2** delight, fight, flight, fright,fortnight, high, highlight, knight, light, lightning, midnight, might, nigh, night **3** twilight, bight, thigh, midnight **4** False, True, False, False **WK** Teacher **GK 1** William Bligh **2** They are all knights.
R1	38	**1** cone, fake, tame, tone, zone **2** school, explain, scream, crawl, appear, fake **3** Teacher **4** frail, coop, tame, fake, tone, zone, green, scream **5** float, tame, frail **WB** taming, tamer, tamed, tamest screaming, screamer, screamed greener, greenest explaining, explained faking, faker, faked needing, needed frailer, frailest

Spelling Matters—Book 3 (3rd Edition) Answers

Unit	Page	Answers
R2	56	**1** their, there, worth, list, child, crush **2** brink, chicken, fling, mend, tram, prong **3** crush, mend, tram **WB 1** worthless, children, stockade, shockwave, blacklist, thereabouts **2** stocking, shocking, listing, crushing, gnashing, plucking
R2	57	**1** Teacher **2** block, child, list **3** prong, pluck, fling **WK** Teacher **GK 1** pope **2** three **3** Eureka Stockade
25	58	**1** Teacher **2** apples, beads, clubs, frogs, races **3** monks, packs, apples, bones **4** goals, frogs, races **WB** hotplates, backpacks, cuphooks, bullfrogs, toffeeapples, nightclubs
25	59	**1** tricks, queens, trains, plates, pests, clubs, races, beads, hooks, scouts,bones, goals **2** apples, bones, hooks, frogs **3** Teacher **WK** queens, pests, apples, serenades **GK 1** frogs (or toads) **2** cheques **3** 60 points
26	60	**1** Teacher **2** buses, riches, rushes, bosses, ashes, torches **3** losses, misses riches, boxes **WB** passed, passes buzzing, buzzes rushed, rushing itched, itching, itches boxed, boxing, boxes washed, washing, washes
26	61	**1** washes, buzzes, misses, torches, witches, boxes, rashes, buses **2** crosses, buses, witches **3** bosses, boxes, buses, buzzes **4** Teacher **5** buses, boxes, passes, bosses **WK** riches, radishes, buses, witches, buzzes **GK 1** radishes **2** The Ashes
27	62	**1** Teacher **2** cries, ladies, babies **3** cries, fairies, stories, flies/babies/puppies/ ladies/daddies/mummies/fairies, parties **4** mummies, puppies, daddies, parties **WB** babies, puppies, flies, cries, parties, fairies
27	63	**1** *Across:* 1 diaries 4 babies 6 parties 7 stories *Down:* 1 dairies 2 ladies 3 daddies 5 cries **2** puppies, babies, fairies, flies **WK** Teacher **GK** puppies, cubs, lambs, foals (colts/fillies), kittens (bunnies), caterpillars
28	64	**1** Teacher **2** boys, toys, joys, bays, clays, rays **3** plays, rays, days, keys **4** trays, keys, donkeys **WB** birthdays, sickbays, highways, paydays, roadways, X-rays
28	65	**1** boys, monkeys, keys **2** Teacher **3** days, bays, ways, rays, trays, plays, clays boys, toys **WK** plays, days, keys, decoys **GK 1** drays **2** monkeys **3** bays
29	66	**1** Teacher **2** fizzes, gases, grasses, pushes **3** kisses (punches), dishes, catches **WB** wished, wishes fizzing, fizzes punched, punching, punches
Unit	**Page**	**Answers**

Spelling Matters—Book 3 (3rd Edition) Answers

Unit	Page	Answers
29	67	**1** punches, glasses, catches **2** Teacher **3** glasses, dishes, foxes **4** foxes, grasses, kisses, punches **WK 1** atlases, cutlasses, screeches, ostriches **2** kisses, wishes, pushes, screeches **GK 1** Teacher (they attack and kill young livestock and fowl) **2** rabbits, wild cats, goats, pigs etc. **3** They are all grasses.
30	68	**1** Teacher **2** bellies, cherries (berries), worries, bullies, armies, rubies, pies **3** armies, bodies, cherries, gullies, jellies, replies **4** lollies (accept also cherries and berries), jellies replies gullies, rubies **WB** raspberries, blackberries, strawberries, cranberries, loganberries, blueberries, brambleberries, boysenberries, gooseberries
30	69	**1** bellies, cities, lollies, rubies, spies, worries **2** bellies, replies, lollies **3** Teacher **4** Teacher **WK** Teacher **GK** spies, berries, gullies, cities, rubies
R3	70	**1** Teacher **2** brushes, clashes, daisies, roses, valleys **3** ponies, lilies, clouds **4** beans, clouds, donkeys, valleys **5** daisies, roses, lilies **6** clouds, classes, clashes **7** donkeys, ponies clouds brushes **WB** baked beans, water lilies, paint brushes, storm clouds
R3	71	**1** clouds, brushes, fairies **2** Teacher **3** classes, donkeys, clashes, ponies, boxes, roses **WK** beans, fairies, studies, valleys, clashes **GK 1** 200 **2** clouds **3** donkeys
31	72	**1** hear, here won, one rode, road, rowed **2** meat, meet, sun, son,weak, week, tail, tale **3** sore, four, see **4** two, too, to **WB** seaside, sailboard, reindeer
31	73	**1** Teacher **2** rowed, rode, road **3** deer, sail, sun **4** Teacher **5** four, sore, here **WK** steak, bear, steal, horse, grate, waist **GK 1** ark **2** Greece **3** tide
32	74	**1** rainbow, backbone, seasick, blowfly **2** Teacher **3** blowfly, weekend, snowball, seasick, outback, cowboy **4** lookout, postcard, see-saw, trapdoor, upset **WB** roadway, railway, highway, pathway, freeway, laneway, alleyway, byway, waterway
32	75	**1** backbone, bushfire **2** ice-cream, sunrise, bushfire, weekend, snowball (rainbow), postcard, lookout **3** Teacher **WK** air conditioner, toothpaste, skateboard, jellyfish (Teacher) **GK 1** spiny anteater **2** bagpipes **3** bushrangers
33	76	**1** I'm, we've, don't, she's, they're, I've, he's, I'd, we'll, you're, we're, I'll **2** Teacher **3** don't, we'll she's you're I'm **WB** she's, don't, we've, we're, I've, we'll, they're
Unit	**Page**	**Answers**

Spelling Matters—Book 3 (3rd Edition) Answers

33	77	**1** we've, we'll, don't, you're, she's, I'd **2** Teacher **3** I have, they are, we are, he is, I am, I will **4** don't, We'll, you're, he's **5** wouldn't, could've, wasn't **WK** we've, we'll, they're **GK 1** Goldilocks **2** seven dwarfs
34	78	**1** dear, fair, fly, bark, ring, light, row, pen **2** duck, duck, bowl, bowl **3** kind, lie, trip, kind, pick, pick **4** Teacher **WB** lapping, freedom, kindness, bowler, tripping, picking, penned, lighten
34	79	**1** *Across:* 2 fair 3 bowl 5 dear 6 kind 7 lap 9 like 10 light *Down:* 1 free 2 fly 3 bark 4 trip 7 lie 8 ring **2** Teacher **WK** light, bowl, fly, light, fly, bowl **GK 1** crane **2** cricket **3** bound **4** fleet
35	80	**1** backfire, backyard, daydream, fortnight, outlaw **2** airport, pipeline, spaceship **3** fairytale, peacock, footstep, tiptoe, homesick, toadstool **4** outside **5** woodwork **6** False, True, True, False **WB** Teacher (outback, background, piggyback, backlog, backup, backlight, backstreet, backstroke, backbone, backstage, backward, backwoods, backhand, backfire, backdrop, setback etc.)
35	81	**1** fortnight, playground, spaceship, woodwork, fairytale, airport **2** tiptoe, sunshine, bushwalk, homesick **3** Teacher **WK** lighthouse, butterfly, grasshopper, keyboard, silverfish **GK 1** They were all bushrangers. **2** chopsticks
36	82	**1** don't, he's, I'd, I'll, we'll **2** we're/we are, I'm/I am, they're/they are, you're/you are, we've/we have, he's/he is, I'd/I had **3** Teacher **4** they're, I'll **WB** I have, you are, do not, I am, they are, she is
36	83	**1** *Across:* 1 they are 5 she is 7 we are 8 I will *Down:* 2 he is 3 you are 4 we have 6 we will **2** I've, I'm, I'd, don't **3** *Do:* a, b, f *Don't:* c, d, e **WK** we're, we've, we'll I'll, I've, I'm, I'd don't, doesn't, didn't you're he's she's they're **GK 1** cheetah **2** elephant **3** blue whale **4** humming bird
R4	84	**1** here, sail, there/their, week, we've **2** row, pen, well **3** bushfire, football, weekend, bedroom, cupboard, rainbow **4** they are, do not we have **5** Teacher**WB** weekend, well-known, overhear, weakling, therefore, sailboard, unwell
R4	85	**1** sail, rainbow, pen, football **2** hear, here sale, sail There, their, they're we've, weave **3** Teacher Notes **WK 1** they have, you have **2** cupboard, afternoon **3** Teacher **4** Teacher **GK 1** Saturday, Sunday **2** sty **3** red, orange, yellow, green, blue, indigo, violet